THE SABBATH AND THE GOSPEL

FINDING REST IN THE COMPLETED WORKS
OF CHRIST

KEITH T FERGUSON

KEITH T. FERGUSON BOOKS

TABLE OF CONTENTS

Printed in the United States of America
Second Printing, 2019

ISBN-13: 978-0692141540
ISBN-10: 0692141545
(Electronic)

ISBN-13: 978-1792617966
ISBN-10: 1792617968
(Print)

Published by Keith T. Ferguson Books
Rockville, MD, USA

❀ Created with Vellum

DEDICATION

This work is solely dedicated to and written for the glory of God the Father in the face of Jesus, the Christ and Son of God, by the power of God the Holy Spirit. I am grateful that God has saved me by His tremendous and sufficient grace. I am also grateful that, through this same grace, God's purposes for His glory are manifestly intertwined with His purposes for both my good and my joy in Him. And so it is for all who trust Him. Amen.

PROLOGUE

This book is about finding rest—true rest. From beginning to end, the Bible addresses and follows the thread of many themes. One of them is rest. That is, it tells of a fallen and restless humanity at last finding an ancient rest in its Maker and Savior.[1]

For me, it has certainly been a process of discovering and further coming to grips with that rest. This process accelerated when my rudimentary understanding of something called "the Sabbath" was abruptly confronted by the Bible's problematic (for me) presentation of it. Seeking answers to a challenging question—see chapter two—eventually brought me to an understanding, a posture, and an application of rest that I had neither experienced nor encountered before. It has been a life-changing journey for me, and I desire no less result for any reader. Before we address the nuts-and-bolts of this book, I want to first invite you to glimpse some of this work of God in my own heart.

.   .   .

A Personal Note of Reflection

The process of biblical exploration and the resulting genesis of a book idea took place during our family's years in Kansas, between 2010 and 2013. However, I didn't start writing the manuscript until 2014, while living in Seattle, WA. At that time, I was less than one month into the process of starting a new church in one of the most under-served and "unreached"[2] cities in North America. I started writing and, despite what felt like a litany of ideas, stopped after only about two chapters. I just didn't have the energy to write it. In the end, I believe it wasn't completed until several years later for reasons that only God saw at the time. To give you an idea of why, I have included below select portions of the original preface for the book, written on February 21, 2014, which reads a bit like a journal entry:

Rest. I need rest. As I sit in a coffee shop in the Beacon Hill neighborhood of Seattle—the desired location of our future plant—I think on the many times I have felt overwhelmed at the task ahead of us. I understand that nothing can be done apart from Jesus Christ (John 15:5), so when something great happens here in our midst, it will have been due to His power and His alone. At the same time, I also know that we have a role in the work that He wants to do here. After all, the same verse speaks of a disciple "bearing fruit" for Him.

So, how do I abide in Jesus, but also bear fruit for Him?

I know that God wants to reach Seattle (along with ALL the nations of the earth) with the Gospel, but how does He want to use me in the process? What if I mess it up? What if I get in the way? What if I miss something? What if I don't pray enough? What if I don't share the Gospel concisely enough, or thoroughly enough? What if I am not a good enough leader? What if I neglect and bring harm to my family in the process? What if our risking everything that we own results in our losing everything that we own? These questions swirl in my head on a regular basis.

I need rest. By now you know that I don't mean a nap. I mean the type of rest that Jesus spoke of: "rest for my soul" (Matthew 11:28-30). I feel that there is a hunger in my soul to know what this true rest looks and feels like. This is why I am writing this book. I want to understand this rest.

I can still see in my mind's eye, the scene on the inside of Victrola Coffee Roasters, with me sitting at the computer—a cold, wet, cloudy, and overall-gloomy day outside the window.[3] I remember sitting there and typing. And I vividly remember the state of my heart and mind at the time. I really did love Jesus. It was a flawed love, no doubt, as is the case with anyone who belongs to Him by faith. We still wrestle our sin and the flesh in this life. Nevertheless, it was still a genuine love. And I also knew that my life was not my own, but His. I understood what Paul reminded the Christians of Corinth long ago, that I was "bought with a price" (1 Cor 6:19-20). As such, I genuinely wanted to honor God. But, something was wrong.

There was a kind of restlessness in my heart that I didn't see at the time, one that God would faithfully bring to light during our family's three-and-a-half years in Seattle. This restlessness was one that didn't necessarily disqualify me or my work, but it certainly did rob me of a lot of joy. And God would faithfully address the need at the right time

After merging our young church plant, Ekklesia Seattle, with another, The Hallows Church West Seattle, we experienced a lot of the fruit for which we had prayed. It was not perfect, but it *was* a beautiful church with such sweet, Jesus-loving people. The church's elder team was composed of loving and humble and brave men, whom I love and respect dearly. We had a great staff team that loved one another and worked well together. We had an awesome church-partner network, composed of churches that gave generously and of leaders that I had grown to love deeply —they were with us and for us and behind us all the way. We were gaining real traction in the community as a genuine and credible witness to faith in Christ and His glorious grace, through the Gospel. Our worship was incredible, our preaching was soul-feeding, and our community was life-giving. In many ways, it was a "dream" scenario for a pastor . . . except that I was restless, and I was tired.

In the months that followed, God performed some unbelievably painful—though very freeing—surgery on my heart. He revealed some ugly insecurities and tendencies within me that had to be dealt with, especially because they were crippling my ability to love, trust, and rest in Jesus by faith. At some point, I was so weak in believing God's love for me, I started *supplementing*—which, in the end, is really only *replacing*—the Gospel with my works. The role I held, the influence I exercised, the gifts I possessed . . . they all became crutches in life to prop-up the objective truth that God loved me.

Slowly-and-subtly, the Gospel of God's grace, forgive-ness, and love was getting harder and harder to believe. It was easier than ever to believe the lie that God was against me because I was so weak, and I kept messing up. I was becoming more and more prone to harshness toward my wonderful wife and my precious children when I felt provoked—God, forgive me! In these moments of deep,

deep heart excavation, God was bringing my heart back to the Gospel and back to true Sabbath rest in Him. I do not have the words to describe how painful this process was (and still is) for me, nor to describe how necessary.

Of all the moments that God would use for this tremendous sanctifying work, none was clearer than when He revealed to us that we needed to take an extended break—to take a Sabbatical. It was somewhat similar to an addict that can only break his or her addiction by removing the drug. It was time for God to remove us from the work of ministry for a season. We had served Him in various capacities around the world for ten years, yet never took an extended break to focus specifically on refreshing our bodies, minds, and hearts in the love of God and in His Gospel. It was very clear that the time was at hand to do so.

Humanly speaking, however, the timing could not have been any worse. Remember, this was a "dream" scenario. And I was in the midst of a heavy battle of trying to feel better about myself and about God's love for me by performing and producing for Him. This was not the time to walk away—yet, it was. It was the perfect time. It was time to walk away and to practice Sabbath on a larger scale. It was time to reduce my productivity and my performance to zero, and to let God love me and my family. And this scared me. For starters, I had never done it before. But, in addition, I was scared of what I would see in myself and of how God would respond.

So when we officially made the decision on December 31, 2016, to resign at some point in 2017, I physically felt a sort of vacuum open in my heart. The heart-mining of God had finally unearthed the cavernous hole inside that had yet to be touched by His faithful, grace-filled, and unrelenting love. It was the next step in this process of laying down my idols, dying to self, and allowing God to purify my worship and my joy in Him. It had to happen. There was no alternative. As such, it makes far more sense that this book be written during a Sabbatical, and not a moment sooner. Not only did I simply lack the energy, but God's providence spared me from the hypocrisy and sin of writing a book about Sabbath and rest in the complete work of Christ, right when I was in the throes of restless idolatry and self-righteousness.

By speaking this way, I do not mean in any way to tarnish the love, work, partnership, edification, and glorification that God graciously produced during our time in Seattle. God is the Master at knowing how to take broken vessels, shape them, and use them even while they are works-in-progress. In fact, I believe this open confession of my weakness brings even more glory to God for what He was able to accomplish, despite my frailties. The Apostle Paul, after asking God on three different occasions to remove a "thorn in the flesh" from his life, heard the divine reply, "My grace is all you need. My power works best in weakness," and therefore concluded, "I am glad to boast about my weaknesses, so that the power of Christ can work through me." (2 Cor 12:8-9, NLT)

I praise God for this testimony of His enduring love and care. Although I was weaker than I ever imagined, I have learned more than ever before—and need continue to learn—how strong and faithful He is. I once heard a quote by A.W. Tozer that effectively states,

> *The devil, things, and people being what they are, it is necessary for God to use the hammer, the file, and the furnace in His holy work of preparing a saint for true sainthood. It is doubtful whether God can bless a man greatly until he has hurt him deeply.*[4]

I would be foolish to presume that God has used me greatly, as I will leave that up to Him to purpose or judge. I only mention the quote because I feel as though I understand how true it is far more than I have before.

There is a visceral and experiential aspect of knowing God that cannot be learned from the pages of a book.[5] To clarify, we *do* need God to reveal things to us intellectually and even conceptually. But, like the great Rabbi He is, Jesus has made it so that lessons are best cemented into our being by experience. The same goes for Sabbath.

I believe that God had numerous purposes for our time in Seattle—as He does in every season of our lives—many of which I may never know. But one purpose I am certain of is that He has made me to understand Sabbath rest more than I was previously able. He gave me just about everything I could have wanted—that is, in terms of ministry and profession and (to some extent) reputation—but it wasn't enough to really satisfy. I knew that only He could satiate my hunger and quench my thirst. I had experienced this truth on various levels in the past, but the time was ripe for a new level of understanding. I knew that heart-rest was essential to life and faith and health in union with Christ. But time and experience has shown me just a little more how true that is. And I'm grateful for it.

On the Book's Author

Moving on now, let's just get this next part out of the way. I am a nobody who, very thankfully, is loved by the most important Being in all of existence: the God of the Bible. On this earth, I know only a few so-called "important" people of some renown—humanly speaking, that is. And of those few people I do know, it is entirely possible that any or all of them are ten times more qualified and skilled to write a book than I am.[6]

Speaking in this way, I seek a sincere posture of humility before readers because I am in need of much grace, as we all are. I am sobered not only by my own history with sin, both before and after I became a Christian, but also by the reality of James 3:1, which says, "Let not many of you become teachers, my brethren, knowing that as such we will incur a stricter judgment." As such, please remember that I am a product of the same grace and of the same Gospel into which I am calling readers to find rest and refreshment. That is, as J.D. Greear fittingly put it, this Gospel that we must all trust in "is not just the diving board off of which we jump into the pool of Christianity; it is the pool itself. It is not only the way we begin in Christ; it is the way we grow in Christ."[7]

On the Book's Origins

In the beginning, I felt compelled to write this book, if for no other reason than to simply get it out of my head.[8] I have no desire to reinvent the wheel or, more plainly, to rewrite that which someone else has already written. However, upon completing the first draft, I came to believe that perhaps this book could be a meaningful contribution —even if only *marginally*—to the existing catalogue of books addressing the topics of the Sabbath and the Gospel.

As a brief aside, regarding this "catalogue of books," the hard work and content of some authors has been incorporated into this book where appropriate or helpful, with great effort on my part to give them every due acknowledgement for their work. Where I have failed to do is entirely unintentional. It should also be noted that I have varying degrees of familiarity with the authors I have referenced and/or quoted in this book; that is, I am more familiar with some than with others. Therefore, readers should not assume that I am intimately acquainted with every position held by every author on every theological matter. Corresponding to this, my sincere appreciation for each author's skillful, referenced work is not necessarily a wholesale endorsement of *all* of his or her written works.

Back to the matter at hand, I praise God that the effort to write this book eventually became both a delight and an issue of faithfulness. I got the sense that God gave me a work to do, and I needed to be faithful and diligent to perform it, regardless of the outcome. All told, I give Him the credit. Should this book prove to be a fruitful work of His great grace, I would get the undeserved honor of pointing to Him as the Giver. It would be a joy to know that a handful of saints were encouraged by the work, or maybe that a few of those who are skeptical of faith (of Jesus, of the Bible, etc.) might be compelled to truly seek and truly find. What a joy it would be to know that God, being the Source of any good thing, allowed any blessing to come through such a weak vessel as I.

On the Book's Length and Content

I assume that many people are like me: really busy and have very little time for books. Therefore, outside of biographies, I prefer books that are "mercifully short."[9] It made sense to keep this work as short as possible, including short chapters, so long as it was also detailed enough to be helpful. This also means that readers need give pardon ahead of time for any theological "rabbit holes" that I chose not to run down, or for any ideas that I chose not to further develop.

Not many written works are truly comprehensive.

Neither will this book be concerning the Sabbath or the Gospel. That would be impossible. Therefore, let us just call this work a *primer*—a book to get the proverbial wheels turning on the Sabbath, the Gospel, and the relationship between them. To explore this relationship, a number of other topics and examples are mentioned, but neither will any of these be comprehensive. Therefore, readers, please approach this work with a spirit of grace, allowing the points to speak for themselves, without over-thinking why certain elements may or may not be present. In one way or another, it was more than likely due to my choice to keep the book mercifully short.

On the Book's Arrangement

There is an intentionally heavy theological emphasis throughout the book, with just a couple of chapters addressing practical matters near the end. The reason for this is that, among those in my relatively small circles of influence, I have encountered more people struggling with the *why* of Sabbath more than the *what*. Of course people still struggle with the *what*, but mostly out of a misunderstanding of the *why*. In many ways, we're all like children, constantly asking "why" when we encounter something. A friend and former colleague of mine once instructed me that, "Healthy doctrine should naturally lead to healthy practice."[10] It is my hope and my prayer that, by spending a disproportionate (but necessary) amount of time on the front-end learning *why* Sabbath is so important to God, the *what* will make more sense and practicing it will come more naturally and joyfully to us.

This work intentionally and carefully starts in the Old Testament and builds into and through the New Testament, so that the matters of the Sabbath and its relationship to the Gospel can be developed with integrity, following how it was developed in the Bible. There will be limitations to this work, but I genuinely want for us to discover and understand what God was really after when He spoke (so frequently) about the Sabbath.

On the Book's Audience

I would love for people of all backgrounds and walks of life to be positively affected by this work. However, I suppose that those readers who have had at least some religious exposure, especially to the teachings of the Bible, will be the most likely to find it accessible. More than anyone, I believe practicing Christians—is there any other kind?—will find the contents of this book useful and edifying. Nevertheless, some real value (and even a surprising sense of freedom) can still be gleaned by the "de-churched" or the disillusioned, or even by those with little-to-no prior experience with Jesus or the Bible. In any case, I am grateful to know that all readers will at least encounter the Gospel within the pages that follow.

Regardless of where you are coming from, I humbly ask you to read on. Should you do so, please read to the end. For starters, no one enjoys being misunderstood, especially those who take the risk of putting their crazy ideas into print. But, more importantly, the chapters are meant to fit together like pieces of a puzzle. By the time you get to the end, the "big picture" will make a lot more sense. So, please take the journey with me and discover what the Sabbath and the Gospel is all about.

1

THE SABBATH AND THE GOSPEL, PART 1

"Remember the Sabbath day, to keep it holy." (Exodus 20:8)

This book is for tired people. I have met few people, if any, who do not experience a degree of restlessness in life, at one point or another. Perhaps it is hard to pinpoint, but there is just some general, persistent fatigue that hangs over us. Maybe you've known this about yourself for a while now, or perhaps the opening line of this book provoked first-time awareness.

Regardless, I am willing to bet that you are somewhere on the spectrum of restlessness, somewhere between a very pronounced and disruptive form of it and, on the other end, a lingering and gnat-like version. Being "at rest" may seem so far away from you that to think of it is despairing; or, the pursuit of rest may be frustrating and exhausting because it always feels only just beyond the touch of your finger tips.

Rest has often eluded me, as I am sure it has you. But, what if it didn't have to be that way?

What if there was a way to truly be at rest? What if there was a way to practice rest, day after day, for the remainder of your days on this third rock from the sun? What if, in the times that you failed to be at rest, there was a way to find it again? And what if finding it again could be done without the expectation that it all depended on *you* —i.e. your strength, endurance, intelligence, moral flawlessness, thoughtfulness, resourcefulness, and so on.

Does that sound like good news? It does to me.

But, like all good news, what makes it truly good is often illuminated against the dark backdrop of bad news.

The Sabbath Defined

It starts with a simple command from God: "Remember the Sabbath day, to keep it holy." (Ex 20:8; cf. 16:23) Have you ever stopped to think about this commandment? I mean, *really* stop and think about it? Think about what it means? Think about how you may (or may not) have heard it taught and/or applied throughout your life? If you have heard of it before, it probably had at least a little bit to do with some kind of rest. Perhaps you grew up in a part of the world where businesses were closed one day a week because of some recognized holy day. If you grew up in the United States, you might remember a time when a number of businesses were closed on Sundays due to it being a common day for worship.

While the occurrence of the word (or the idea of) "Sabbath" does present itself quite prominently in the Book of Exodus, it appears for the first time much earlier in the Bible. In fact, it appears at the beginning, in Genesis 2:2. And, interestingly, it doesn't describe what man does but, rather, what *God* does.[1] The more specific Hebrew word *shabbâth*[2] (Ex 16:23; 20:8) comes from the root word *shâbath*, which the *Dictionary of Biblical Languages* defines as, "[to] stop, cease, be still, be quiet, i.e., have an activity no longer continue".[3] In other words, the very essence of the Sabbath, whatever it is, involves one stopping, ceasing, or quieting.

The Sabbath Commanded

The context of Exodus 20:8-11 provides a helpful starting place for contemplating the Sabbath. This portion of the Bible is well-known as "The Ten Commandments." Generally speaking, the scene involves the God of the universe giving commands to a specific group of people, the Israelites, by way of a chosen spokesman, Moses. A few observations might benefit right away. First off, if we're talking about a supremely good God—and the Bible clearly and repeatedly emphasizes this as a quality He possesses—every other command among "the Ten" makes perfect sense, doesn't it? Start with the commands about God and then move on to commands about people, and they reflect a sense of moral goodness to them.

For the Christ-follower, it is reasonable to conclude that the worship of other gods is evil (Ex 20:1-6). And, if this God of the universe is worth all honor and affection, of course one shouldn't regard His name lightly and "take it in vain" (20:7). Honor your father and mother (20:12) . . . sure.[4] Do not murder (20:13) . . . absolutely. Do not steal (20:14), do not lie (20:16), and do not desire what belongs to others (20:17) . . . check, check, check. It makes sense. They even appear to "descend" in order of importance, so-to-speak, from honoring God down to honoring fellow humans. One might even say that they all fit into a neat little package for those who love tidy catch-phrases like,

"To follow Jesus means to simply love God and love your neighbor." Each clearly has its place among the Ten . . . except for one: the fourth one. That would be the one about keeping the Sabbath.

Why is it there? How does it fit? What does it *really* mean?

By and large, I have encountered a great deal of confusion about the Sabbath and what it means. If you do an internet search about it, a wide variety of answers and viewpoints awaits you. Some can be rather vague and possibly unhelpful, proposing that practicing Sabbath means to essentially take a break or take a day off from work every now and again to get some rest—there is hardly any framework involved. Others consider the day a rigid and specific demand for rest from all habitual, daily activities such as work, study, and even leisure. Some maintain that it is an archaic practice because religion in general is archaic, or conclude that religious rules have no consequence for those who self-identify as irreligious. While others assert that the significance of Sabbath has been nullified because the Law of God has been invalidated by freedom in Christ. In this particular instance, it may even be said that "Christ is the end of the law for righteousness to everyone who believes" (Rom 10:4).

Bad News, Meet Good News

This ambiguity is dangerous, especially in a world full of restless people. After all, according to the Old Testament Law, God *commanded* anyone who would be called by His name to set apart and practice Sabbath as holy. It wasn't optional; it was mandatory. And, as we will explore in the next chapter, the penalty of violating God's command of Sabbath was death. Taken at face value, therefore, the command to remember and practice Sabbath—no matter how good God's intention for it—has actually become a source of death to anyone who takes His Law seriously.

You might be thinking, "Wait, I thought you said there was good news?" There is! That good news is the Gospel.

The word for Gospel in the original New Testament language of Greek was *euangelion*, which means "good news" or "good message."[5] This Gospel says that Jesus Christ, the Son of God, perfectly fulfilled the Law of God without a single error. According to the plan and purpose of God, Jesus took this perfect life and this perfect fulfillment of God's Law, and He willingly gave Himself up to the point of death on a criminal's cross in order to satisfy the justice that God demanded for the offense of our sinful essence and of our blatant moral failure. However, God then raised Jesus up from the dead, bodily alive forever, as the capstone of completion on the work that was necessary to save us from sin, death, and hell—the work that was necessary to bring us back to Himself. In short, one might say that a great exchange took place: "He made Him who knew no sin to be sin on our behalf, so that we might become the righteousness of God in Him." (2 Cor 5:21) Anyone who repents of (turns from) their sin and trusts this Gospel by faith will be saved (Rom 1:16-17).

And now you might be thinking, "But what does this have to do with the Sabbath?" Great question!

The Sabbath and the Gospel

The purpose of this book is to communicate a very simple and very clear message. I want readers to sincerely study the Bible, and come to this conclusion and conviction: *The Sabbath is a gracious gift from God. Its primary purpose is to point the world to the Gospel—to both prepare the heart for it and to cultivate life in it.* Naturally, such a concise statement deserves more explanation.

Readers will observe in the ensuing survey of the Scriptures that there is more than enough compelling evidence to conclude that the Sabbath indeed points to the Gospel, and it does so by communicating that:

1. there is a work of some kind that desperately needs to be done;
2. we are utterly helpless to perform it;
3. God is not only perfectly able to complete it, but He has already done so or promised to do so;
4. as a result of His promised or completed works, God's people are to assume a posture of rest in every facet and season of life; and
5. if there is any subsequent work to which God has called His people, it is to be performed only from that posture of rest.

Coming to this conviction about the Sabbath has profound implications for how we live our lives and on how one can positively impact the world. *The regular practice of Sabbath reminds us of our great need for the rest that only God can give; it encourages others among the people of God; and it gives credible testimony to a restless world in dire need of the Gospel.*

It's All about Jesus

My prayer is that readers come to this conclusion about the Sabbath and the Gospel because I believe this is the conclusion at which *God Himself* wants us to arrive. The Bible is God's inspired, inerrant, and infallible word to the world and it points its students in this direction. Reading and studying the Bible with Christ-centered lenses leaves us with no other outcome. We will find no reading as restful, as vibrant, and as life-giving as one that tightly knits together the Sabbath and the Gospel.

The reason for this is because it is all about Jesus, the One who voluntarily and lovingly worked and completed for us what we could not do for ourselves. He both fulfilled for us and delivered to us the righteousness of God, apart from and because of our utter inability to arrive at it in our own strength. Or, as Sally Lloyd-Jones eloquently puts it for both little readers and big, "[T]he Bible isn't mainly about you and what you should be doing. It's about God and what he has done."[6] The Bible is all about Jesus, as is the Gospel and the Sabbath.

I tremble at the thought of believing so boldly because I fear coming across in any way as arrogant, as a know-it-all, or even as self-deluded. Nevertheless, if we are truly meant to see Sabbath in this light, that is, in the glorious light of the Gospel, then it is absolutely essential that we change our views, teachings, and practices surrounding it. In failing to see the Sabbath as pointing to, preparing for, and cultivating life in the Gospel, people are literally being robbed of life and joy and (perhaps in some cases) even salvation.

2

THE DEATH PENALTY AND THE SABBATH

"Therefore you are to observe the Sabbath, for it is holy to you. Everyone who profanes it shall surely be put to death; for whoever does any work on it, that person shall be cut off from among his people. For six days work may be done, but on the seventh day there is a Sabbath of complete rest, holy to the Lord; whoever does any work on the Sabbath day shall surely be put to death." (Exodus 31:14-15)

This section of Exodus changed everything for me. I had been practicing Sabbath as best I knew how for years, but the journey of understanding the Sabbath took a significant turn here. The moment I read this and began to comprehend for the first time the weight of what God was communicating, I could not view the Sabbath in the same way anymore. No longer could it be viewed somewhat haphazardly. No longer would a fairly vague interpretation be good enough. I had to know more.

Not long after the Sabbath is introduced in Exodus 20,[1] there is a severe and grave penalty applied to any infraction: the death penalty. Read that sentence again. When it finally struck me, I couldn't believe what I was reading. According to my understanding of the Sabbath at the time, it seemed unwieldy, inconsistent, and even petty of God to bring such a hefty penalty against what I thought was so small an offense. After all, think about the times in the Bible that God assigns the death penalty.

In fact, let us take a quick look at only *some* of the instances found in *just* Exodus and Leviticus.[2] God handed down the death penalty to His people for murder (Ex 21:12, 14 and Lev 24:17, 21); for the physical abuse of one's parents (Ex 21:15); for verbally cursing one's parents (Ex 21:17 and Lev 20:9); for human trafficking (Ex 21:16); for gross negligence that directly leads to the death of another person (Ex 21:29); for sexual activity with an animal (Ex 22:19 and Lev 20:15-16); for worship of other gods (Ex 22:20); for oppression of the helpless, e.g. the widow and orphan (Ex 22:22-24); for child sacrifice (Lev 20:1-5); for sexual infidelity in marriage (Lev 20:10); similarly, for inappropriate sexual activity with other family members (Lev 20:11-12, 14, 19-20); for homosexual activity (Lev 20:13); for the practice of witchcraft (Ex 22:18 and Lev 20:6, 27); and for blasphemy against God's holy name (Lev 24:16).

While those I have listed may not be universally agreed upon, it is worth noting that many (if not most) of them have been historically considered gross moral and even *legal* infractions in numerous cultures around the world.[3] That being said, is it not interesting that Exodus 31:14-15 lists the violation of Sabbath as among these mortal offenses against God and humanity? And, in the event that 31:14-15 was not clear enough, the sentencing can also be found in 35:2, among other places.

· · ·

Is God Cruel?

If understanding and practicing Sabbath amounts to basically taking a break from everyday activity, or, as some perceive it, God's chummy suggestion to "take a nap" every now and again, then why is a violation of it so absolutely and violently punishable by death? If I am a Jewish person who lives under the Law, but forgets to take a nap on this special day, or who decides to go ahead and clean up the living room, why do I deserve the death penalty?

If this unclear and undeveloped understanding of Sabbath is the reality, then the corresponding death penalty would be worse than sheer exacting punishment. In fact, it would far surpass such cruel and inhuman practices as removing the thief's hand for stealing a loaf of bread.[4] It would be beyond unfair. The punishment wouldn't fit the crime. If this were so, how could a so-called holy, just, and loving God lay down such an apparently severe, coldhearted, and unjust punishment for so small an infraction? Not only would it be unfair, it would be inconsistent of God.

However, when one reads through this section of Exodus and Leviticus, there is an inherent and obvious fairness when God is dealing with offenses. In the Old Testament, we see an example of this in the idea of restitution. Suppose an animal was wrongfully (or even intentionally) killed or stolen by someone; in such cases, the penalty was often restitution. The person simply had to "make it right" by paying back what was lost, plus a little more. By comparison, to intentionally kill an innocent person was murder, or to steal them was human trafficking, both of which were punishable by death. A New Testament example of this type of valuation is found in Jesus' teaching from Luke 12:6-7. Here, to make a point about where one's fear ought to truly lie, Jesus compares the value of sparrows to the (far greater) value of people. This is because people are made in God's image, and animals are not. So, an offense against an animal is certainly wrong, and God sees this; but an offense against a person, an image-bearer of God Himself, is abundantly worse.[5]

God Wants Our Attention

Now the point of all this is that, if we're smart, and in this book we will at least *pretend* to be so, perhaps we should give God the benefit of the doubt here and assume that He is unquestionably in the right on this one. That is, for now at least, let us assume that God is not being cruel or unfair when He initially laid down the death penalty for violating the Sabbath. He must have had some very good reason to do so.

For the sake of argument, we will believe that God has something He wants to communicate to us about Sabbath by assigning such great importance to it. And, if that is indeed the case, then it is already clear that something about our understanding of the Sabbath needs to change. There is something in the eyes of God that we are missing about the intentions of Sabbath, to the extent that our violation of its remembrance and practice is deservedly punishable by death under the Mosaic Law.[6]

But what could we possibly be missing? This will become clearer as we move along.

We will revisit this matter of the death penalty later on in chapter six, "Mt. Sinai and the Sabbath." However, at this point, it is more essential for us to move forward by going back to the very beginning.

THE CREATION AND THE SABBATH

"By the seventh day God completed His work which He had done, and He rested on the seventh day from all His work which He had done. Then God blessed the seventh day and sanctified it, because in it He rested from all His work which God had created and made." (Genesis 2:2-3)

I f we truly want to understand what the Sabbath is all about, it is necessary to return back to the first time it was mentioned or described. The triune God of the Bible was at work in Creation over the course of six days (Gen 1:31). In addition to this, the Scriptures state that, after these six days of creation, the work was unquestionably good (1:31) and definitively completed (2:1). And, in case those details were unclear or misunderstood, the declaration of the completed nature of the work and the six-day duration taken to complete it are both restated immediately afterwards: "By the seventh day God completed His work which He had done" (2:2). Further, we may also recall various other mentions of this in Scriptures. The six days, the completeness of the Creation, and the rest of

God are all plainly spoken of again by God Himself in Exodus 20:11; 31:17 and Hebrews 4:4, 10, to name a few.

Perhaps this sounds redundant or over-emphasized, but the importance of this to understanding the nature of the Sabbath is essential. To put it plainly, we must clearly understand that God *finished* His work in creation. It was *complete*.

The Completeness of Creation

Think about how many projects have been started in human history, with details having been forgotten or neglected and later revisited. Imagine your last attempt to take a road trip. You probably spent extensive time planning, packing, loading, etc. Undoubtedly, however, the moment you were only ten miles on your journey, you realized that some item or detail was forgotten and you were left wrestling with whether or not it was worth it to turn around.[1]

We can't even take a simple trip without forgetting even some major detail like locking the front door of the house or turning off the coffee maker. Imagine the vastness of creation—atoms, gravity, trees, mountains, oceans, people, white blood cells, taste buds, planets, atmospheric conditions, moons, solar systems, orbits, stars, galaxies, the entire universe—and then ponder on the fact that not one thing was missing. Not a single thing was out of place. God had completed this work with utter perfection.

He surveyed the whole of creation and found that, in His infinite wisdom and power, nothing was lacking and everything was good. There is a staggering sense of rest to that scene, isn't there? Everything was complete. Everything was good. Everything was as it should be. And everything that would ever be needed was already present. This was such the case that God had the freedom to rest on the seventh day. The presence of rest was an indication of completion. God could have left that part out of the Bible, but He didn't.

Try to picture humanity's parents, Adam and Eve,[2] in that serene state of true utopia. At any point, can you imagine them looking around and thinking that something essential was missing? Or, that something still needed to be added? Even if you entertain that something was possibly missing, can you imagine a situation where these creatures (who were made from the dust), are actually in a position where they could do something about it? If they actually have enough knowledge to recognize that something was missing, do they even have the power to bring about such a material change? And where would God be in all of this? Would He be sitting idly by, thinking about how glad He is that people were around to complete what was so clearly lacking in His creative efforts? "How foolish of Me to think I was done with my work," God might say, "but I am so glad that Adam and Eve were here to point it out to Me! Otherwise, there might have been some real trouble!"

Sounds absurd, doesn't it? And that's the point.

It was perfect because God made it so. Everything was in order because God made it so. Everything was beautiful because God made it so. Everything was genuinely good because God made it so. And what makes it all the more astounding is that He seemed to do it effortlessly, with only the sweet sound of His voice.[3] The stark beauty we read about in that world is an infinitely far cry from the world that we know today. In fact, it is so different, that people have a hard time believing that the Genesis account is true. After all, how could such a good world have become so rotten?

Something must have happened. But what?

4

ADAM AND EVE AND THE SABBATH

"The Lord God planted a garden toward the east, in Eden; and there He placed the man whom He had formed. . . . Then the LORD God took the man and put him into the garden of Eden to cultivate it and keep it." (Genesis 2:8, 15)

Their names were Adam and Eve, and they were clearly the *pièce de résistance* of God's astonishing creation. They were the *magnum opus*, the greatest and most important creative work-of-art of this Artist-God of the Bible. They were made in His image (Gen 1:27-28); they basked in His glorious presence in the garden; and they enjoyed an unbroken and unhindered relationship with Him. There was no such thing as sin, evil, guilt, or shame. There was only goodness, only love, and only beauty. The simple mention of it triggers the soul's longing for rest, for a return to that home to which we originally belonged.[1] If we take the time, we can learn a lot about God's plan for Sabbath when we observe His dealings with humanity's parents, especially in a world not yet tainted by rebellion.

If Genesis 1:1–2:3 portrays a sort of "30,000 ft. view" of the creation event, then Genesis 2:4 appears to mark the transition to a more "zoomed-in" description, especially of day six and the creation of man and (eventually) woman. After forming the man from the dust of the ground (2:7), we read that "the LORD God planted a garden toward the east, in Eden" (2:8) and that He "took the man and put him into the garden to cultivate it and keep it" (2:15).

So we see that, before any trace of sin entered into God's beautiful world, there was real work to be done. Don't be mistaken, though. This work was not God's already completed work of creation. Nevertheless, there was work to do in this new world.[2] Adam was given the task of cultivating the garden (2:15). We also see him given the task of naming the creatures that God had made (2:19-20). Eventually, Eve is added in order to complete the equation (thank you, God!) and these tasks are presumably taken-on by the both of them.

God Works First

At this point, recall again the clear organization of Genesis 1:1–2:3. Six days of creation are followed by a seventh day for rest. The focus of the text is entirely on God and His ability to create all things with just the power of His words. Everything in existence occupied the passive role; all things were being acted upon and were being created. God was the active figure in creating; everything else was inactive. God created in six days, and then He rested on the seventh. As was carefully described in the previous chapter, God did all the work—all of it. As it pertains to the specific act of creation, we can conclude that Adam and Eve could add nothing to the work that

God had performed—not one thing! Again, the reason why is because it was already finished; it was already completed (2:2).

This leads to another conclusion about the specific act of creation. All of the work that Adam and Eve would perform in the garden was, therefore, not *in order to* complete it but, rather, *in light of* it having already been completed. Their participation with God in His created order was simply coming alongside something that He had already finished. As those created in the image of God, they were now going to practically express it by cultivating and keeping (2:15) that which God had already made.

Another way the Bible puts it is found immediately following the verse pertaining to the creation of Adam and Eve: "God blessed them; and God said to them, 'Be fruitful and multiply, and fill the earth, and subdue it; and rule over the fish of the sea and over the birds of the sky and over every living thing that moves on the earth.'" (1:28) In some circles, this has been deemed as the "creation mandate" or the "cultural mandate." God appointed people to be the stewards of creation, as it were. God made it and God owns it, but humanity was to manage it in a way that reflects the Creator and His intentions.

As many saints have said, written, etc. in times past and present, the various cultures throughout history and all over the world have the sacred opportunity—rather, the expressed mandate—to steward and maneuver the elements of creation in innovative ways that respect their Creator, as well as the image of God in themselves and in others. Words, music, minerals, art, gardening, food, clothing, family, and so much more can all be freely utilized and formed according to this command from God.

· · ·

Man's First Work is Rest

All of this leads to yet another important conclusion, which we observe in God's activity to place or put Adam (and eventually Eve) in the garden to cultivate and keep it. We see the word "placed" or "put" in both 2:8 and 2:15. The instance in 2:8 simply means something along the lines of "to put, place, or set" in the Hebrew language,[3] and it is an entirely different word than the one that is used in 2:15. The word used in 2:15 is highly significant as it pertains to Sabbath because it comes from the verb "to rest." As K. A. Mathews describes the word, "'Put' in v. 15 translates the causative form of the verb *nûah*, 'rest,' and so could be rendered literally 'caused to rest.'"[4] In other words, the specific wording used in Genesis 2 indicates that Adam was "caused to rest" in the garden by God, and only *after* which was Adam to work, cultivate, and keep it.

The basic sentiment of *placing* in 2:8 could have easily been repeated for 2:15 but, instead, a different word was chosen. What is significant about this is that 2:8 has no indication of Adam's work; in fact, this does not appear until later in 2:15. It is also interesting to note that the very next verse (2:9) reveals God as *causing to grow* everything in the garden. Therefore, we see that God is "causing [Adam] to rest" before the mention of the work assigned to him. His very presence and rest in the garden was the result of God's activity and, similarly, Adam's work would *proceed from* God's work and rest.

Accordingly, Adam (and Eve by extension) did not perform one single bit of the work until *after* God actively "caused [him] to rest" in the garden. The first activity in which Adam and Eve engaged in this new world was not work, but rest. Read that again: Adam and Eve's first action in this new world that God created was not work, but rest. And, to be even more precise, they were enjoying the rest that God Himself enjoyed.

Consider these words from a deceased brother-in-Christ, Watchman Nee, who briefly touched on this concept in his book, *Sit, Walk, Stand*. It is a beautiful summary of what we have labored over in this chapter:

> *Adam, we are told, was created on the sixth day. Clearly, then, he had not part in the first six days of work, for he came into being only at their end. God's seventh day was, in fact, Adam's first. Whereas God worked six days and then enjoyed His Sabbath rest, Adam began his life with Sabbath; for God works before He rests, while man must first enter into God's rest, and then alone can he work. Moreover it was because God's work of creation was truly complete that Adam's life could begin with rest. And here is the Gospel: that God has gone one stage further and has completed also the work of redemption, and that we need do nothing whatever to merit it, but can enter by faith directly into the values of His finished work.* [5]

The theme of rest has tremendous importance throughout the Bible, and the pattern is there from the very beginning. God works and afterward, having completed His work, He rests. Humanity, being benefactors of this completed work, must first share in God's rest before participating in the work assigned to them. Adam and Eve would take up the work of cultivating and keeping the garden, but not until after they first enjoyed the rest that God Himself enjoyed as a result of the work that was already completed by Him. And, when it came time for them to work, because God's work of creation was already complete, their work would be a different kind altogether.

This sounds nice, doesn't it? However, what we've

concluded certainly doesn't seem to describe the world that we live in, does it? To understand further, we must also explore where it all went wrong, where rest became a fleeting thing for the children of men.

5

THE FALL AND THE SABBATH

*"Therefore the L*ORD *God sent him out from the garden of
Eden, to cultivate the ground from which he was
taken. So He drove the man out; and at the east of the garden
of Eden He stationed the cherubim and the flaming sword
which turned every direction to guard the way to the tree of
life."* (Genesis 3:23-24)

A dam and Eve possessed the perfect world that
everyone dreams of, and they let it slip through their
fingers. When God placed them in the garden, He gave
them a rather tremendous amount of freedom. "You may
freely eat the fruit of every tree in the garden" (Gen 2:16,
NLT), God says, with only one stipulation: "except the tree
of the knowledge of good and evil" (2:17a, NLT). To make
sure they understood the weight of His words, He even
warned them of the consequences of any failure to trust
this command: "If you eat its fruit, you are sure to die."
(2:17b, NLT)

As a brief aside, it's funny and rather absurd that we
often read this part of the Genesis story and then think to

ourselves: "Why did God forbid eating from one of the trees? Who is God to restrict them (us)?" We completely overlook the fact that, outside of that one restriction, God gave His children nearly absolute freedom in His new world. They had so few restrictions, so much freedom to enjoy, and we like to focus on the single restriction and its consequence. But, perhaps I digress. . .

Naked but Not Ashamed

Well, as many know the story from Genesis 3, God's enemy came and tempted Eve, who eventually ate fruit from the forbidden tree, and she then gave some to Adam, who also ate (3:1-6). This is where it all came crashing down. When this happened, it is not in the least a coincidence that the very next words in the Bible are, "Then the eyes of both were opened, and they knew that they were naked. And they sewed fig leaves together and made themselves loincloths." (3:7, ESV) It may sound like a very strange series of events, but its importance is paramount, especially when one considers the words immediately prior to this whole devastating scene: "And the man and his wife were both naked and were not ashamed" (2:25).

This nakedness described in Genesis, believe it or not, represents something that every person on planet earth craves—whether past, present, or future. This is not a creepy or sleazy desire for nakedness that we're talking about. This nakedness was very literal, but it is also highly symbolic. For just about everyone, you will be hard-pressed to find a more vulnerable situation than when you're naked before someone else. Perhaps we are ashamed of some part of our bodies; or maybe we bear the scars of some prior abuse or betrayal; or there can even be a sense of shame that has crept in due to the memory of prior reckless activities with our bodies. Regardless, again, the meaning is much deeper. Believe it or not, there is a way for a people to be emotionally "naked" with another person, or to be intellectually or relationally "naked," and so on.

This points to one of the greatest fears in the human experience: to be fully-known (i.e. "naked" in every sense of the word) but afterward rejected. Timothy and Kathy Keller, in their book on marriage, explored the deeply-human and vulnerable issues of acceptance, rejection, and being known. They concluded that:

> *To be loved but not known is comforting but superficial. To be known and not loved is our greatest fear. But to be fully known and truly loved is, well, a lot like being loved by God. It is what we need more than anything. It liberates us from pretense, humbles us out of our self-righteousness, and fortifies us for any difficulty life can throw at us.* [1]

This is one of the reasons why we wear masks and put up walls and show pretense. We are terrified to show who we really are and, subsequently, find that we are unacceptable before those from whom we crave acceptance.

A brief but noteworthy example of this is how there are many studies that show how psychological damage is done to children when they face rejection in the home. As we know, the home is the very first place where people are meant to experience positive human interaction, love, acceptance, safety, protection, and care. When those experiences are negative, the damage is deep, lasting, and very difficult to overcome.

This is what is at stake when Adam and Eve are standing buck-naked before one another and, get this, before God the Creator, Himself. Before the God of the universe, they were fully exposed and naked in every literal and symbolic sense that the word can evoke. But, as we read, they were at first not ashamed by it. There was no need to be. It was a perfect world, and they carried not one internal blemish of sin, guilt, or shame; nor did they bear any outward blemish in physical health. This is what it was like for God to look upon the whole of creation and call it "very good." It is very difficult for us to comprehend this because it is so far from our human experience. But this is truly what it was like for Adam and Eve, as well as what it was *meant to be* like for us, their descendents.

But, it did not last.

Desperate for Covering

The serpent lied to them, subtly, but still masterfully, and they bought into the lie, failing to believe what God had previously and unambiguously told them. Once they did this, the first reaction was to notice their nakedness and attempt to cover it. This means that they were now ashamed as they stood completely naked and exposed before one another. There was now a glaring shortcoming in their humanity that wasn't there before. In response to this, they made clothes out of leaves. There was a huge problem, and they tried to fix it. Even if they had succeeded in covering up their vulnerability before one another, there was now another and even bigger problem.

In those days, God used to walk in the garden in the cool of the day, among His creation and His creatures (3:8a). Adam and Eve, face-to-face with their own naked-ness and shame, now made an effort to hide themselves from the presence of their Maker (3:8b). If there was anything in the Genesis account to indicate how far and how fast they had indeed fallen, it was this. For the first time ever, humanity was now hiding from God. And it has been that way ever since. How tragic.

As a result of this catastrophe, God hands out consequences (3:14-19) for all parties involved: the man, the woman, and the enemy (disguised as a serpent). When you read through those consequences, especially to Adam and Eve, the inherent bliss and restfulness of that new world evaporates in an instant. Worst of all, it concludes with this staggering statement about death: "By the sweat of your face you will eat bread, till you return to the ground, because from it you were taken; for you are dust, and to dust you shall return." (3:19) It seems like all hope is lost, doesn't it?

God Provides Clothing

If you blink, you will miss that there is a glimmer of hope found in this section. Buried within God's pronouncement upon the serpent is a rather interesting promise: "I will cause hostility between you and the woman, and between your offspring and her offspring. He will strike your head, and you will strike his heel." (3:15, NLT) God makes mysterious mention of a descendent that will come from the woman. Just as humanity will have conflict with this enemy, so will this particular descendent. This descendent will be "struck" on the heel by the serpent, but will in turn "strike" the head of the serpent. It is worth noting that if you're trading blows with someone, an injury to the head is a lot worse than a blow to the heel. In fact, one can be lethal, while the other almost certainly cannot.

Therefore, even though Adam and Eve could not overcome this serpent, in the midst of genuinely ideal conditions, no less, it seems that one of their descendents will. The enemy that brought them down would be brought down by one of their offspring. In order to bring a bit more clarity into the picture, we will reflect on this from Adam and Eve's point of view: "We are now at war with this serpent. But in the future, someone like us will come and do what we could not. We lost the conflict with God's enemy, but this descendent will win." This was an absolutely essential work, but it was also one that Adam and Eve themselves had already proven unable to perform. That being said, take a moment to ponder this question: *Of all the characters in this drama, who is the only one that is capable of doing what Adam and Eve were unable to do?*

We find our answer near the end of this scene: "The LORD God made garments of skin for Adam and his wife, and clothed them" (3:21). Why would God do this? Didn't Adam and Eve already cover themselves? There would be no need for God to do this, that is, unless He considered the work of Adam and Eve as insufficient to cover their nakedness. Evidently it was. Their efforts to cover up that which was now symbolic of their personal guilt and shame were not good enough. Therefore, God stepped in and did it for them. To add to the intrigue of the scene, He performs this work with animal skins, which makes one wonder, "Where did He get those from?"

To answer this, recall God's promise to His image-bearers about eating from the tree that was clearly off-limits: "in the day that you eat of it you shall surely die" (2:17b, ESV). Did God lie? After all, Adam and Eve are now walking around in animal skins, and God is about to send them out of the garden. That doesn't sound like they're dead. Sure, they will die one day. Some time down the road, they will for certain return to the dust, but that's in the future. The result of all of this disaster in Genesis 3 appears to lack the urgency and the immediacy of the warning in 2:17, which indicated that death was going to be imminent if there was a violation.

True to His word, but paradoxically in an unexpected turn-of-events, God does indeed kill something. However, it clearly wasn't the two who were at fault. In order to cover up guilt, shame, and the *insufficient work* of Adam and Eve, it appears that God instead kills an animal and uses its skin to cover them. It was the first substitutionary death in the Bible, and a necessary one at that, but it would not be the last.

6

THE EXODUS AND THE SABBATH

"You shall remember that you were a slave in the land of Egypt, and the Lord your God brought you out of there by a mighty hand and by an outstretched arm; therefore the Lord your God commanded you to observe the Sabbath day." (Deuteronomy 5:15)

When one reads or recalls the story of Israel's deliverance and exodus from slavery in the land of Egypt, the concept of Sabbath doesn't typically come to mind. I have rarely, if ever, heard the two linked together. Perhaps that is due to the fact that it doesn't really seem to show up in close proximity to the event itself. However, this does not mean that they two are not intimately connected. Bible verses like Deuteronomy 5:15 remind readers that the exodus event is pregnant with a great deal of meaning, including as it relates to the pattern of Sabbath that was established in Genesis 1-2.

A Desperate Situation

To explain, let's set the scene: The Hebrews have been in captivity for more than 400 years in a foreign land, Egypt. The circumstances of their initial mass migration and arrival to the land were actually quite good. It was part of God's plan to preserve the family of Jacob, also known as "Israel." Surrounding the rather challenging story of Joseph was a providential plan to save the family of Israel by bringing them to Egypt in the midst of famine (Gen 45:1-13).

Interestingly, this whole series of events was even promised two generations prior, when God spoke to Abram/Abraham about it (Gen 15:13-16). According to the sovereign plan and purposes of God, this man's descendants would spend four centuries in a foreign land; they would rapidly increase in numbers; and they would be fatally oppressed by the host nation. However, God would eventually rescue and deliver them and then take them to a land of rest.

So, imagine the nation of Israel: a giant nation composed of slaves being oppressed by another nation. And it was not just any nation; Egypt was the world's greater power in those days. To curb any possible attempt to free themselves with their sheer numbers, the Egyptian leadership initiates a horrific population control method that involves killing all the newborn baby boys within Israel (Ex 1:15-16). As time goes on, the burden of their slavery gets progressively worse. Even when God reminds them of the promise of deliverance, they are a broken people with no hope of delivering themselves. The oppression has sunk so deeply that there is no hope for them . . . that is, unless God intervenes and does something about it.

Again, there are many themes and lessons from the exodus event, but one of them is that Israel was in a help-less, enslaved, and defeated state and in desperate need of

God to act on their behalf. Otherwise, bondage and hope-lessness and death would be their enduring reality.

Only God Can Save

This is the part where Moses comes into the picture, as well as the ten plagues, etc. If you've never read or listened to the story all the way through in one sitting, I encourage you to do so now. It really is incredible. And, as you do so, be encouraged to observe at least two things of enormous importance. First, note how many times God says something like this, "But, indeed, for this reason I have allowed you to remain, in order to show you My power and in order to proclaim My name through all the earth." (Ex 9:16) Secondly, note how many times the story emphasizes either directly or indirectly that God is the One actively doing *all of the work* to rescue Israel from the land.

Be sure not to miss how *inactive* Israel is in the midst of the numerous and wondrous plagues that take place all around them. Pay attention to how they are protected from all of them. Take notice of how the one, true, and living God works so powerfully on their behalf, without them having lifted a finger to save themselves. These helpless Israelite slaves not only leave Egypt in celebration, but they also plunder the Egyptians of all their goods (Ex 3:22; 12:36). Unbelievable, am I right? Except that it's true.[1]

If that weren't enough, there is also the matter of the Red Sea. It seems as though God is really, really, really trying to make a point. The Israelites partied their way out of Egypt and then everything suddenly comes to a full-stop at the edge of the Red Sea. The same Pharaoh who just sent Israel out of his now decimated nation, has a change of heart and sends his chariot horde after these former slaves to destroy them—they will pay for what just took place in his land. He is going to make up for the utter shame and disgrace that his nation experienced when the God of Israel comprehensively overpowered and embarrassed him, along with the gods of Egypt.[2]

The scene at the Red Sea is the climax of the story that involves some wild combination of jubilation and rage, victory and defeat, hope and despair. Could you imagine what would have happened to the Israelites if Pharaoh caught up to them and God had not intervened? It would have been a bloodbath. The Israelites knew it, too, which is why they were panicking. They were losing their minds, even in such close immediate proximity to the great deliverance of the exodus. And they were even losing hope in the presence of a supernatural pillar of cloud (by day) and fire (by night) which they had followed out of the land (Ex 14:1-12). To put it another way, one does not get to the end of the exodus event and think, "Israel really handed it to those Egyptians, didn't they?" No way.

God Works for His People

The God of Israel is the Hero, and this God comes through in the face of circumstances that seem impossible for humanity. Moses would tell the people,

> *Fear not, stand firm, and see the salvation of the LORD, which he will work for you today. For the Egyptians whom you see today, you shall never see again. The LORD will fight for you, and you have only to be silent.* (Ex 14:13-14, ESV)

Read the account and you will see how this God of Israel certainly did work for and *on behalf of* His people.

The waters of the Red Sea part and become like a wall on their right and left (14:22, 29). Israel walks through the parted sea on *dry* ground (14:16, 21, 22, 29). And, after every man, woman, child, beast, and cart passed through the sea, the waters then cascade down upon the pursuing Egyptian chariots (14:28). It must have been a breathtaking scene to witness, because it certainly can be overwhelming to read. It is no wonder that Israel bursts into glorious song (15:1-21). To that point, do not overlook how God is described as the One performing the activity of salvation. Observe how many times Israel sings something along the lines of, "You, O LORD, did this" and "You, O God, did that."

Perhaps it is time to re-examine the pattern that emerged from Genesis 1-2.

God's people were enslaved and without hope. The work that needed to be done was deliverance, or salvation, from the land and oppression of Egypt. Rescue was clearly a work that only God could do on behalf of Israel, and thankfully it is one that He promised He would do. In the course of this great work, Israel had nothing to contribute. It was completed by the hands of God alone. As a result of this completed work, Israel enjoyed both rest from their enemies and from their oppression, as well as the anticipation of a coming rest in a land promised to their forefathers. As a result of all of this work—God's work—was there any work left for Israel? That is, was there any work to be performed that was based on God's completed or promised work? The answer is "yes."

The Exodus and the Sabbath

Part of the work was faith: "Israel saw the great power that the LORD used against the Egyptians, so the people feared the Lord, and they believed in the LORD and in his servant Moses." (14:31, ESV; cf. 14:13). Part of the work was also the act of worship: "Sing to the LORD, for He is highly exalted. . ." (15:21). However, the response we are especially interested in at this point is found a bit later on in the Bible:

> *You shall remember that you were a slave in the land of Egypt, and the LORD your God brought you out of there by a mighty hand and by an outstretched arm; therefore the LORD your God commanded you to observe the Sabbath day.* (Deut 5:15)

As a result of this already-finished work of salvation and deliverance from Egypt, and as a result of the promise that God would soon take them to a land of rest, Israel was commanded to remember and to practice Sabbath. In fact, the very *means* by which they were to remember so great a salvation and deliverance from slavery was the keeping of Sabbath. In other words, they were to *remember* and *rest* in God's completed work on their behalf. That doesn't sound so bad at all; it actually sounds very wise and kind of God.

But, would Israel obey? Would they rest? How can we know if they did or not? Well, let's just say that the God of Israel is expert at bringing-to-light what is buried in the darkest recesses of the human heart.

Enter the wilderness and the manna.

7

THE MANNA AND THE SABBATH

*"Moses said, 'Eat it [the manna] today, for today is a
Sabbath to the Lord; today you will not find it in the field.
Six days you shall gather it, but on the seventh
day, the Sabbath, there will be none.'"* (Exodus 16:25-26)

Having transitioned from the vibrant wonder and awe
of the Red Sea event to the bleak surroundings of
nearby wilderness (i.e. a desert), it didn't take long for
Israel to lose their way and start complaining again. I can't
say I blame them; I'm pretty sure I would have done the
exact same thing in their situation. In fact, I am certain I
have done the same thing, only with different circumstances. We all have.

Israel is headed toward a land "flowing with milk and
honey" (Ex 3:8), which is a really, really good and exciting
prospect. However, in order to get there, they have to cross
a vast wilderness. If anyone has been camping for more
than one day, you learn pretty quickly that it takes quite a
bit of resources and preparation to survive apart from
one's normal dwelling, routines, and sources of supply for

daily needs. If you have ever been camping with children or "indoors-y" people, because they effectively require the same amount of effort to please in the great outdoors, you stand back and wonder at the sheer amount of things you have to pack.

Now take that, and multiply it by about a million when you consider taking an entire nation traversing across a wilderness. Understandably, one of the first realizations that the people of Israel have is, "How are we going to survive out here?" They are literally helpless to attend to their own survival. Consequently, it is no small wonder that they panic when they are confronted with the fact that they have no water supply to carry with them along the way to the end of their journey (Ex 15:22-27). Despite their groaning, however, God is gracious and miraculously provides for His people.

Afterwards, the people have another occasion of panic: "What are we going to do about food?" In response to this, God says He is going to "test" Israel's faith (i.e. their willingness to remember and to rest in His promised care and provision) by sending bread to the earth every day (Ex 16:14). That is, every day except for one: the Sabbath.

In the Shoes of a Sojourner

Imagine you are an Israelite with kids and other dependents to feed, but you're in the middle of the desert. [And, while we're at it, don't forget that the precariousness of "hanger" is not a new thing. It was every bit as real back then as it is today, except they did not have the gift of a SNICKERS® bar to help address it.][1] You've seen God provide water, which was actually pretty amazing, though, it did leave you sweating a bit; it felt a bit too close for comfort. Now, you need God to provide food as well. You get word that food will indeed come, but by way of a sort of bread "rain" that will be ready for gathering every morning. *Are You sure about this, God?!* Nevertheless, you give it a try and decide to trust Him to provide.

The first morning arrives and you find the bread-like substance on the ground. There you go! God provides for the needs of the day. Then, next day, same thing: God provides. A couple of days in, you realize that God meant what He said in that each day would provide enough supply for that day only. To drive home the point, any leftovers from the night before fester with worms and a putrid smell (Ex 16:19-20)! In all, you see God faithfully provide every single day for five days in a row! But, now there's a problem. Or, at least, it seems like a problem. Food will come tomorrow, but *not* the day after.

God said that He will not send bread on the seventh day because it is a day for remembering the Sabbath (Ex 16:25-26). Therefore, you are to gather and prepare twice as much on the sixth day in preparation for the seventh day. On that day, the Sabbath, you are neither to gather nor to prepare anything. That seems well-and-good, I suppose. But imagine how it might have felt to wake up that seventh day and see nothing on the ground. In the midst of what felt like desperate circumstances, you were relieved and reassured to see manna every day for those first six days. But now there is nothing.

I can only imagine the host of Israel nervously eating the remaining morsels of food that were prepared on the day before: "Okay, this is pretty wild. Our leftovers from every single other day turned into *[pauses to wretch]* something rather malodorous and disgusting, but now our leftovers smell and taste as good as fresh. What gives? Oh, and now there's nothing on the ground. How do we know something will be there tomorrow when we wake up? How can we be sure?"

Rinse. Lather. Repeat.

This process would take place for what ended up being forty years in the wilderness. That could not have been easy, to say the least. It must have been a terribly painful crash-course in trusting God, one that necessitated the experience of death to the human tendency towards self-reliance. Nevertheless, this was the weekly practice for this wandering band of former slaves.

As it was from the very beginning, God meets the needs of His people by performing a work that only He can do. In this instance, He miraculously and faithfully provided for and sustained a helpless nation in the middle of a wilderness desert. God promised several times beforehand that He would fulfill that work. Considering how reliable He has been so far in this story, a simple promise should be considered as good-as-done, right? That is, in a sense, the work is already-and-not-yet *complete*. It may not be completed in the chronology of humanity's timeline just yet, but it certainly is in the mind of God, which in itself should be more than enough for our certainty. And, as a result of the promised-and-therefore-already-completed work of God, what is Israel supposed to do? What is the work that they are to perform?

They are to listen to the voice of God. They are to Sabbath. They are to rest.

8

MT. SINAI AND THE SABBATH

"Remember the Sabbath day, to keep it holy. Six days you shall labor and do all your work, but the seventh day is a Sabbath of the LORD your God; in it you shall not do any work, you or your son or your daughter, your male or your female servant or your cattle or your sojourner who stays with you. For in six days the LORD made the heavens and the earth, the sea and all that is in them, and rested on the seventh day; therefore the LORD blessed the Sabbath day and made it holy." (Exodus 20:8-11)

Many present-day explanations of Sabbath have been formed from the events of Mt. Sinai. It is a significant aspect of the narrative, of course. As was discussed in the first two chapters, the command for Israel to Sabbath was prominently placed within the Ten Commandments (Ex 20:1-17) and violation of the command was to be met with no less than the death penalty (Ex 31:14-15). However, we have also been shown from the Bible that Sabbath was revealed well before the events at Mt. Sinai. If that's the case, then why is there confusion over the importance of Sabbath?

Salvation by Grace, through Faith

Before proceeding any further, it is essential to make something very clear. Any time the Law of God is discussed, it is of utmost importance to also pause and say a word about *grace*. I articulate this because humanity is, due to our sinful nature, prone to these things: idolatry (i.e. false worship), self-reliance (i.e. false strength), and self-righteousness (i.e. false salvation).

Therefore, on one hand, if I start listing a bunch of *do's* and *do not's* about how to relate with God, readers will naturally desire to pull out notepads, build a checklist, and try to save themselves by way of personal performance. We will swiftly take our eyes off of the sufficiency of our Creator and put them squarely on ourselves. Or, conversely, we will altogether change the list and, in turn, create a new god that aligns more with our own personal desires and preferences. Neither way is how it works with the one, true God of the Old and New Testaments.

Concerning this, we read very clearly within the Bible:

God saved you by his grace when you believed. And you can't take credit for this; it is a gift from God. Salvation is not a reward for the good things we have done, so none of us can boast about it. (Eph 2:8-9, NLT)

From the beginning of time, the lesson is that we are brought into relationship with God by way of faith in His promises and in His provision. Hebrews 11 provides a very clear picture of how men and women of old, well before the incarnation and work of Jesus Christ, were made right with God through their faith, even if they had to believe promises shrouded in more mystery than we can comprehend on this side of history.

At this point in time, however, much has been revealed about God's promises and, as such, the requirement upon people entails a *very specific* faith in the death, burial, and resurrection of Jesus Christ, the Son of God, who performed this work on our behalf. Full stop. The reason for this: "There is salvation in no one else, for there is no other name under heaven given to people, and we must be saved by it." (Acts 4:12, HCSB) Since there is "no other name" by which we can be saved, there is no possibility of self-salvation. This most assuredly cancels out our performance and efforts to please God. It's all about Jesus and *His* perfect ability to please God the Father and, by His atonement for sins, save us forever and ever (Heb 7:25). Faith is our point of entry, as well as that which keeps us.

Now that we have firmly established this, we can now return back to the Ten Commandments.

Disregard for the Sabbath

Why are we so comfortable teaching the present-day legitimacy of "you shall not murder," while at the same time disregarding the Sabbath? The same goes for theft, adultery, idolatry, and so on. What is it that has led many followers of Jesus to pay little or no attention to the Sabbath, whether explicitly through teaching or implicitly through practice? Though one should be careful of speaking in absolute terms, there appears to be a palpable disregard of intellect towards and affection for this command among churches and Christians—it sure looks this way in my home country—to the extent that we treat it as optional in the eyes of God.

What is especially insidious about this is the potential that exists for religious hypocrisy. We may speak of the command's importance, but foolishly do nothing notable or distinct to demonstrate the divine value of rest in the midst of a restless world. Or, we may attach a number of auxiliary commands to it, calling others to follow our lead, while fully incapable of keeping them ourselves. On the other hand, perhaps in our ignorance, we might insist that the Sabbath is no longer important because we now "live under grace;" but subsequently, we get bent out of shape and become ungracious with people who believe that it really does still matter. Any of these ways is perilous for our thinking, our affections, and our practice.

The Death Penalty: Revisited

Consider again the matter of punishments levied against people for certain offenses. If God is just, and keep in mind that we are *at least* assuming that He is, then it seems reasonable to follow that the sins which offended God the most were the ones that resulted in the death penalty. The penalty for robbing God of His glory (i.e. idolatry) was far more severe than the penalty for robbing a family of a goat (i.e. theft). Certain offenses resulted in a period of ritual uncleanness; some in restitution; while others necessitated an animal sacrifice.

If you think about it, ultimately, each of these involves a sacrifice of some kind. While any sacrifice (by definition) is costly to one extent or another, some things are clearly more costly to forfeit than others. And one can forfeit no greater thing than his or her own life. So, again, why is the relevance of Sabbath disregarded so quickly, especially when we consider that failure to observe it resulted in the loss of one's life?[1] The point of these words is not to promote the idea of a religious nation-state where those in authority get to lavishly hand out the death penalty like its Halloween candy. No! Instead, the point is to drive into our hearts the inherent significance of the command.

Before we spend any more time plumbing the depths of the Sabbath, what it means, and why we should practice it, we must at least be willing to accept that it is still important to God and, thus, still essential for our well-being. If we are going to point to Exodus 20 and insist that these matters: faithful worship of God, faithfulness within marriage, honor for one's parents, and respect for the property of others, are truly good in the sight of God and worthy of exercise, then we must likewise speak and practice the same with regards to the Sabbath.

Try to think about this in light of the biblical narrative we've been exploring. How problematic would it be if Israel forgot where salvation came from? How destructive would it be for Israel and, more importantly, for God's glory manifested in and through His people? Given the inclinations of the human heart, how easily would it be for Israel to forget? How likely would they be to neglect the practice of Sabbath? Why is this issue such a big deal?

Profaning the Sabbath is Profaning the Gospel

The willingness to disregard this command is nothing new. And, as much as I am aware of (and even express) my sins and those of my nation, I also understand that these are age-old problems of the human heart, including among the roaming band of Israelites long ago. God was establishing a new nation, one that would live distinctly among the surrounding nations. He would do so in order to make them like a beacon in darkness, a city set on a hill, to shine light upon the greatness of their God. Seeing that

He's the only God who is able to save, we should not be surprised that He wants to shine the spotlight on Himself, so that other nations can look to Him and be saved as well. This has always been God's heart.[2]

God meant for the Sabbath to point to, prepare for, and cultivate life in the Gospel—the good news of salvation through His gracious and complete work—even in the days chronicled throughout the Old Testament. This link between the Sabbath and the Gospel is the only one that makes sense of this perplexing issue of the Sabbath and the death penalty. God wants to save people, to save the nations of the earth, and when we mess with the Sabbath we are, in effect, robbing ourselves and others of vital knowledge that points to the very heart of salvation.

To put it another way, those among God's people who violated the Sabbath and (worse) taught others to do the same, were denying both themselves and others the opportunity and the ability to be pointed to, prepared for, and cultivated in the Gospel. These would be guilty of abandoning and even profaning God's good news of salvation to the world and also spreading it to others—what a horrifying thought!

Should you happen to disagree with the frightening severity of this, please call to mind these statements from the Bible, some of which are from the lips of Jesus Himself:

> *Then Jesus spoke . . . . "Whoever exalts himself shall be humbled; and whoever humbles himself shall be exalted. But woe to you, scribes and Pharisees, hypocrites, because you shut off the kingdom of heaven from people; for you do not enter in yourselves, nor do you allow those who are entering to go in."* (Mt 23:1, 12-13)

> *He [Jesus] said to His disciples, "It is inevitable that stumbling blocks come, but woe to him through whom they come! It would be*

better for him if a millstone were hung around his neck and he were thrown into the sea, than that he would cause one of these little ones to stumble." (Lk 17:1-2)

But even if we, or an angel from heaven, should preach to you a gospel contrary to what we have preached to you, he is to be accursed! As we have said before, so I say again now, if any man is preaching to you a gospel contrary to what you received, he is to be accursed! (Gal 1:8-9)

These verses (among others) tell us that, firstly, it is a dreadfully foolish and terrifying thing to forget and/or abandon what God says about His salvation and how to receive it. Furthermore, it is exponentially more bone-chilling to be found a source of stumbling for someone else in these matters, to the extent that such a one is now hindered in their ability to understand, believe, and receive God's good news to the world. Yikes!

It may surprise some to hear that there is more than one way to reject God and the Gospel. Timothy Keller, in his book *The Prodigal God*, explores the parable convention-ally known as the "Parable of the Prodigal Son" (Lk 15:11-32). Along the way, he leaves readers with a number of rather insightful conclusions, one being:

Jesus' message, which is 'the Gospel,' is a completely different spirituality. The Gospel of Jesus is not religion or irreligion, morality or immorality, moralism or relativism, conservatism or liberalism. Nor is it something halfway along a spectrum between two poles—it is something else altogether. [3]

In other words, one can try to manipulate and control God—and, as a result, neither *truly* love nor relate with Him—by an outright moral rebellion or by an inward rebellion that is masked by religious fervor. In stark contrast to both of these dead ends, the way of Jesus and His Gospel is entirely different and entirely satisfying.

Our relationship with the Sabbath can be a lot like this. I have seen people (myself included) try to practice Sabbath in such a way that is cold, legalistic, and ultimately self-serving and self-righteous. This obviously is not pleasing to God, nor is it something that points to the Gospel of grace. On the other side of the spectrum, it is also dangerous to outright reject what the Sabbath has to say for reasons described earlier. Neither way is beneficial. Neither way points to the beauty of the Gospel. Therefore, we fully reject both.

We want to arrive at the truth, no less than the "bulls-eye" of what God has purposed to communicate through the giving of the Sabbath. This is at the very least because, as we have observed, it can be a matter of life and death. And, the more we explore the more we will see just how true this is.

9

THE SIGN AND COVENANT OF THE SABBATH

*"The LORD spoke to Moses, saying, 'But as for you, speak
to the sons of Israel, saying, "You shall surely observe My
sabbaths; for this is a sign between Me and you throughout
your generations, that you may know that I am
the LORD who sanctifies you. Therefore you are to observe
the Sabbath, for it is holy to you. . . . For six days work may
be done, but on the seventh day there is a Sabbath of
complete rest, holy to the LORD. . . . So the sons of Israel
shall observe the Sabbath, to celebrate the Sabbath
throughout their generations as a perpetual covenant." It is a
sign between Me and the sons of Israel forever; for in six
days the LORD made heaven and earth, but on the seventh
day He ceased from labor, and was refreshed.'"* (Exodus
31:12-17)

We reflected previously on the fact that we are prone
to idolatry, self-reliance, and self-righteousness. If
we are willing to receive and believe this hard truth about
ourselves, things will begin to make a lot more sense. We
are about to learn from the book of Exodus yet another

facet to the precious significance of remembering God's command to practice Sabbath.

An Ancient Restlessness

We live in a restless world, do we not? New York City, perhaps the most famous city in the world, is affectionately known as "The City that Never Sleeps." Very similarly, Tel Aviv is known as "The City That Never Stops." And Las Vegas proudly wears the title, "Sin City." Advances in technology allow us to communicate with those on the other side of the world in real-time, even for free, as long as there is a strong internet connection. Advances in transportation mean that there are very few places left on earth where humans have not been or cannot get to with relative effortlessness. Growing awareness of worldwide news and financial markets allows us to be more attentive to (and anxious about) the state of our future, both individually and collectively.

More than ever before, we have access to the world's places, people, and information; and we can have what we want with more ease, speed, and regularity. However, despite this, we also appear to be more uncertain than ever before. The population of our spinning globe is rapidly growing—as of the original writing of this sentence, it is approaching nearly 7.5 billion people.[1] Yet, the world somehow and strangely feels so small, and so does our perception of individual worth and significance. With the hands and eyes of the masses regularly glued to smart phones or electronic devices, it entirely feasible to conclude that we are less equipped than ever before to deal with matters like silence, inactivity, waiting, and discomfort.

Here's the catch, though: this is nothing new. This is an ancient problem for the human race. Of course, the technology and various advancements are new; but, the twitchy and relentless ways we use them are merely "fruits" of the inwardly restless spirit shared by us all.

Throughout the ages, we have struggled to slow down and to rest. It was like this even before the days of a freed Israelite nation wandering in the wilderness. We have been prone to and even immersed in busyness, financial worries, being workaholics, and stressing about relationships ever since our parents were "shown the door" out of the Garden of Eden. This fallen world has always been over-worked, overstressed, and under-rested. Today, we have turned our numerous technological advancements, which were supposed to make life a bit *easier* and altogether *better* for us, into an opportunity to cultivate and become enslaved to our restlessness.

But why does this even matter? Why should we care?

Well, it matters because we hate it. These unending patterns of edgy and anxious self-destruction are simulta-neously things that we hate, wanting to be rid of them forever, and also things we cannot seem to give up because we cannot or refuse to imagine our lives without them. The situation is a bit like a crutch. We started using some of these things and developing these patterns as a way to cope with or distract ourselves from life (e.g. dealing with pain), but now we are uncertain how we will ever be able to "walk" once the "crutches" are removed. We wonder, "Can it really be better that this? Will it be worth it?" But, then we quickly reassure ourselves, "No, it's not as bad as I'm imagining it. I'll be fine."[2] We continually find ourselves in this cycle of restlessness that we wish we could escape, but not sure if we *really* want to or if it is worth the pain of adjustment. And it has been this way in every generation throughout history.

Knowing this is true, how distinct would it be if you

met someone who did *not* constantly live like this? Perhaps you already have. If we have, it is possible that we hate them almost as much as we hate ourselves, am I right? We want what they have, and are ominously unsure if or how we will ever get it. But, again, why does this even matter?

It matters because this is the Sabbath that God has called His people to.

Sabbath as a Sign

Note what it says in Exodus 31:12-17, that the Sabbath would represent at least two things for Israel. First, it was to be a "sign" between God and His people. If signs are meant to point or direct someone towards something, what was this particular sign supposed to point Israel to? We read that God gave Sabbath "that you may know that I, the LORD, sanctify you" (Ex 31:13, ESV). God gave His people a continual reminder that He is the One who "sanctifies" them. Well, what does that mean? The *Dictionary of Biblical Languages* defines this Hebrew word *qadash* as, "[to] be sacred; be consecrated; be dedicated; be set apart; and be holy; etc."[3]

To explain, imagine a closet full of clothes. As is the case with almost every wardrobe, each article of clothing has a purpose and an occasion for its selection. Some clothing is useful for mowing the lawn on a hot summer day, while others are reserved for very special occasions. Some are for sleeping and others for exercising. If you were going to attend a wedding, would you wear pajamas, slippers, and your finest morning breath? No way! You would wear those outfits which are "set apart" for special occasions. The suit or tuxedo you might wear to a wedding might be used for other occasions as well, but they are most likely special (not common) ones. This is only a small, crude, and slightly silly picture of what it means to be set apart *from* the world's purposes and, instead, *for* God's.

God said that the Sabbath was going to signify to the people of Israel that they were "set apart" by Him and for His purposes. That's pretty extraordinary! If you're an Israelite hearing this for the first (or hundredth) time, you're astonished to learn that God chose you out of every nation on planet earth, and set you apart from everyone else for a unique purpose. But, don't miss another important facet of the verse. Did this state of being "set apart" have anything to do with Israel's merit or performance? Again, no way! In fact, the opposite is true. Israel was perhaps least deserving because they were allowed special access to God but squandered, abused, and neglected it over and over again.

We are incensed when we see or hear about people who grew up with immense privilege and status and, subsequently, waste their advantage on utter self-absorption and on maddeningly self-destructive tendencies. Israel was a lot like that in their wastefulness of special access to the one, true, and living God. Nevertheless, this God chose to set them apart. They were utterly useless in and of themselves, but He would still take them and designate them as special among all the nations. That had to be encouraging (and humbling), right? And one of the regular, repeated signs that God gave His people to testify of this reality, both to them and to the world, was the practice of Sabbath.

And that's not all.

The Sabbath was to signify something else, too. It was to be "a sign between Me [God] and the sons of Israel forever; for in six days the LORD made heaven and earth, but on the seventh day He ceased from labor, and was refreshed.'" (Ex 31:17) This is amazing! In case the people of Israel were to forget where this all started, God pointed

them back to the very beginning, to the very origins of
Sabbath: the Creation story.

The lessons, patterns, and insights that one might draw
from the Creation narrative of Genesis were supposed to
flood into the here-and-now in order to serve as a present
and relevant reminder of ancient truths. Sabbath is as old
as time itself, and the very first one was enjoyed by God,
who had just completed His works. It was also enjoyed by
Adam and Eve, and it would serve as the starting place for
the works assigned to them. The regular practice of
Sabbath within the nation of Israel was to remind them of
this, and it was meant to bring them into a posture of restfulness before the God who works on their behalf. As has
already been stated abundantly, and will be even more, the
works of God on behalf of His people are complete and
lacking in nothing.

Sabbath as a Covenant

While "sign" was the first word used to describe
Sabbath, it was not the only word. The other word used is
"covenant." The people of Israel were to "observe the
Sabbath, celebrating it throughout their generations as a
perpetual covenant" (Ex 31:16, HCSB). The Hebrew word
used for "covenant" is *berith*. Again, according to the *Dictionary of Biblical Languages*, this word refers to a "covenant,
treaty, compact, i.e., an agreement between two parties;
pledge, a binding oath of promise"[4]

A friend and former colleague of mine, Andrew
Arthur, helpfully and eloquently described covenant relationship in this way: "It speaks of a mutually beneficial
relationship that is more personal than a friendship and
more accountable than a contract—like what is supposed
to take place in a marriage."[5] The Bible's usage of this

word is pervasive, used repeatedly in both the Old and New Testaments. It is one of the most thematically note-worthy words in all the Scriptures, used most prominently to describe the type of relationship that God creates between Himself and His people. To overstate its impor-tance is literally impossible. Therefore, God is bringing an impassibly weighty word to bear upon the people of Israel when He calls them to practice Sabbath. It is a matter of covenant.

Perhaps it is helpful to think in terms of a interpersonal relationships. Borrowing from the Arthur quote and the language of marriage, imagine Sabbath as a wedding ring. While views on wedding rings may vary widely, these rings have generally borne great meaning in cultures around the world because they serve as tangible reminders of the marriage vows and promises made on the wedding day. A wedding ring simply says, or at least *ought to* say, "I am taken. I joyfully belong to someone else, and that other person joyfully belongs to me, until death parts us!"[6]

The ring I wear to symbolize both my marriage and my vows to my wife, Julie, is precious to me. Though I often fidget with it, I rarely take it off. If there is a circumstance when I have no choice but to take it off, I either temporarily put it on another finger or put it back on my ring finger ASAP. To some, that may seem a bit excessive. But, to me, it makes perfect sense because I have chosen to let my wedding ring have incredible signif-icance for my marriage. When I have felt tempted, I have touched my ring and remembered my vows. When I have felt angry or disappointed, I have looked at my ring and remembered those precious promises. It says to others and it reminds me that I have made a covenant, and I have chosen to be bound to another for as long as I live. By God's grace, I will keep that promise until I die. And, in all of it, the ring serves as a regular and tangible reminder.

As with any illustration, there will be points where it falls short. Nevertheless, this is at least a helpful glimpse of what the Sabbath was supposed to mean and represent in this "marriage" covenant between God and His people. As we will continue to discover, Sabbath is not just a *command* from God to His people, it is also a wonderful *gift*. And in God's marriage to His people, He gives them this precious gift of Sabbath to bear witness to the special status they have in His sight, to the relationship that they share together, and to the precious promises that are reserved especially for them.

Lynne M. Baab writes in her book, *Sabbath Keeping*:

> *The Sabbath is one of those gospel duties that absolutely convinces us of the goodness of God. The more we practice it, the greater a privilege it becomes, the more essential it feels, the deeper it connects us to the river of life that provides fruit in all seasons. . . . The Sabbath teaches us grace because it connects us experientially to the basic truth that nothing we do will earn God's love. As long as we are working hard, using our gifts to serve others, experiencing joy in our work along with the toil, we are always in danger of believing that our actions trigger God's love for us. Only in stopping, really stopping, do we teach our hearts and souls that we are loved apart from what we do.*[7]

I hope that, by now, we are at least beginning to glimpse how unwise we are to neglect the understanding and practice of Sabbath in our relationship with God. If we hold it under the light long enough, we will begin see it unfurl into full bloom and behold its true beauty. In what we have discovered, can we honestly say that this is an oppressive command from a cruel and exacting God?

Instead, what do we see? We see a God who has repeatedly demonstrated that He is the loving and benevolent Author and Perfector of all good works within His creation, especially in His dealings with humanity, and most especially as it pertains to His chosen people. In a restless world, He is the God who offers rest. While the world frets endlessly about the past, present, and future, He is the timeless God who promises His faithful love, care, and provision. The only thing He asks in return is for people to trust Him and rest in Him. And, if there be any specific work for us, the only way it can be done properly is if it flows from out of that trust and rest.

10

THE PROMISED LAND AND THE
SABBATH

*"The LORD spoke to Moses on Mount Sinai, saying, 'Speak
to the people of Israel and say to them, "When you come into
the land that I give you, the land shall keep a Sabbath to the
LORD. For six years you shall sow your field, and for six
years you shall prune your vineyard and gather in its fruits,
but in the seventh year there shall be a Sabbath of solemn rest
for the land, a Sabbath to the LORD. You shall not sow your
field or prune your vineyard. You shall not reap what grows
of itself in your harvest, or gather the grapes of your
undressed vine. It shall be a year of solemn rest for the land.
The Sabbath of the land shall provide food for you. . ."''*
(Leviticus 25:1-7, ESV)

Time would go on for Israel, and they would
eventually enter and occupy the special land that
was promised to them and to their ancestors. It was to be a
land of rest for God's people, especially in light of their
recent slavery in Egypt. While in the land, Israel was to
follow their God and, in doing so, would enjoy the many
good gifts that He would give them. One of those gifts was

Sabbath, and it was so important that it was even to affect how this people went about the work of tending their crops.

A command was given to Israel that, every seventh year, they were to let the land itself rest. They were not to sow seeds or do any other kind of preparation, nor were they to reap any harvest or gather any yield that came from the fields. This is a bit similar to the situation with the manna, but turned up to eleven.[1] Again, put yourself in the shoes of someone who has to care for a family or (more likely) an extended family; and you have just been told that you are to let the land just sit idly for a year. As is the case with any agrarian society, you live and die by the land. And you find out that you have to cease from all working of the soil every seventh year. Wow!

We won't spend a lot of time unpacking this concept, but the key to understanding this command is what has already been explored about the Sabbath, in conjunction with this verse: "But you may eat whatever the land produces on its own during its Sabbath" (Lev 25:6, NLT). Taken in isolation, this verse would make no sense and we would likely disregard it, missing out on all that it has to teach us. However, in light of what we have discovered about the nature of Sabbath, this verse makes perfect sense.

The Death of Self-Reliance

It would have been very easy for those tending the field in Israel to view their success (or their failure) in the fields *solely* as a result of their labor and toil. However, we already know or have learned enough about the God of the Bible to recognize that He is the Giver of all good things, including provision. Remember, that lesson was learned in the wilderness. Yes, Israel would have work to do in their new home. They would do everything they could to care for the land to make sure that they could survive and even thrive, wherever possible.

However, as we all know, when we're successful, we are prone to give ourselves the credit. When we believe our own efforts to be the source of deliverance from any sort of lacking (e.g. economically, relationally, spiritually, etc.), then we tend to trust ourselves more-and-more and God less-and-less. The security and even, by extension, the insecurity of the future becomes dependent on us. This mindset is a cosmic "no-no" for those who want to follow the God of Israel, and it carries with it only the biblical expectation of (self-) destruction.

The God of the Bible is described as the Giver of life. He is also viewed as the great Initiator and Source of all good things. He is the Worker of the impossible, of that which we cannot accomplish in ourselves. He is the One who completes every good work that He begins (cf. Php 1:6). In this conversation about Sabbath, all of these statements must be considered as the bedrock upon which everything else is built, or else the activity and even the commands of God will not be rightly understood.

Therefore, when it comes to the land and to the seventh-year Sabbath for the land, the worker of the field would have to trust God in very profound ways. He or she would have to trust God to be all of these things and more, or else they would not survive the year. And God knows this, which is why He goes out of His way to explain how trustworthy He would be in this scenario:

> *If you wonder: "What will we eat in the seventh year if we don't sow or gather our produce?" I will appoint My blessing for you in the sixth year, so that it will produce a crop sufficient for three*

years. When you sow in the eighth year, you will be eating from the previous harvest. You will be eating this until the ninth year when its harvest comes in. (Lev 25:20-22, HCSB)

Do not miss something central about the trustworthiness of God here. He was already to be viewed as the reason for the survival of His people in years one through six. When they are working hard and succeeding, God is still the Giver of that good thing. He is worthy of Israel's trust in years one through six. What makes year seven any different? Only that was exactly the point. By ceasing and doing nothing in the seventh year, the people of Israel were tangibly reminding themselves of ancient truths—of truths that already existed since the beginning of Creation, long before they ever stepped foot into the land of promise.

This God of Israel is all at once the singular great Giver, Initiator, Source, Sustainer, Worker, and Finisher of all good on behalf of His chosen people. And this truth would never be more evident than when they were regularly and voluntarily choosing to cease their normal activity according to God's commands. If the people of God could somehow learn this lesson in the silence and inactivity of rest and Sabbath,[2] then it would carry forward into daily living and work as well.

And if that lesson were truly learned, then everything would change.

11

THE PROPHETS AND THE SABBATH

". . . all who keep the Sabbath without desecrating it and who hold firmly to My covenant—I will bring them to My holy mountain and let them rejoice in My house of prayer. Their burnt offerings and sacrifices will be acceptable on My altar, for My house will be called a house of prayer for all nations." (Isaiah 56:6-7, HCSB)

Israel lived in the land of promise for centuries and, while there were a few exceptionally bright spots, it was largely a catastrophe. To put it all too briefly, if the relationship between God and His people was supposed to be like a marriage, then Israel turned out to be a lecherous whore. She blatantly cheated on her husband; flaunted it in his face; insisted that she was doing nothing wrong; and had the gall to do so repeatedly, even after having been given a thousand-and-one second chances (Jer 2:22-37).

At the end of the day, her actions explicitly, implicitly, and overall shamefully communicated to the watching nations of the world, "Every other man on earth is better than my husband. He is unworthy of my love and devotion." And, to make matters even worse (yes, sadly, that is actually possible), Israel carried herself about like the worst prostitute you've ever heard of. She would rather steal money from her husband in order to pay customers to be with her, rather than simply be with her loving and faithful husband (Ezek 16:1-34).

That's pretty bad, huh? Don't worry. You and I are no different, so there's that. . .

All the while, God continually warned His people that they were in for disaster if they continued in their unfaithful ways. He sent prophet after prophet and spokesperson after spokesperson to Israel, in hopes that she might turn from her ways and be restored to her God. Along the way, several prophets even mention the Sabbath and call Israel to demonstrate a change of heart by remembering and practicing it.[1]

The Restorative Nature of the Sabbath

Isaiah 56:1-8, in particular, is very striking in this regard. God tells His people that salvation will soon come to them, and that the one who keeps Sabbath is blessed (56:1-2). Even foreigners (non-Israelites) and eunuchs, those who naturally and unassumingly view themselves as cut-off[2] from relationship with God, will be blessed by Him through the remembrance of Sabbath (56:3-7). God will even bring back the outcasts of Israel and more (56:8). God says of these,

> *I will bring them to my holy mountain of Jerusalem and will fill them with joy in my house of prayer. I will accept their burnt offerings and sacrifices, because my Temple will be called a house of prayer for all nations.* (Is 56:7, NLT)

In other words, those who remembered and practiced Sabbath in those days of grief would have joy in the presence of God and in relationship with Him (e.g. in prayer), and will have complete confidence that they are acceptable in His sight.

So, get this: Despite everything that Israel did to pervasively dishonor the name of their God, the one and true and living Creator God of the universe, He chose to extend mercy to them and call them back to Himself. However, in order to do so, they had to remember and practice Sabbath. They had to remember that they have absolutely nothing to offer God in the situation—that is, other than their appalling sin, guilt, inadequacy, and shame—and that they are entirely dependent on Him for restoration.

It is not at all unlike the Creation event. One might look upon God's beautiful new world and rightly consider it foolish to believe that they have any advice or help to offer God in order to make it better and more complete. And it is not at all unlike the exodus,[3] except that this time Israel is in bondage to their sin and to their regrettable past. The people of God have nothing that they can bring to the table, but their God has more than enough in Himself. And He promises to bring it upon His people in the fullest measure.

God has promised salvation to His people, and He is no liar. It is so absolutely certain, in fact, that the recipients of the promise might as well consider it already completed. Since God is truly and graciously going to bring them into His presence again, they have nothing left to do except to believe Him and practice Sabbath, which is why He commanded them to do so . . . in order to be ready for His certain salvation.

12

THE EXILE AND THE SABBATH

"Those who had escaped from the sword he [King Nebuchadnezzar] carried away to Babylon; and they were servants to him and to his sons until the rule of the kingdom of Persia, to fulfill the word of the LORD by the mouth of Jeremiah, until the land had enjoyed its sabbaths. All the days of its desolation it kept Sabbath until seventy years were complete." (2 Chronicles 36:20-21)

The land was going to get its Sabbath one way or another. The message was going to get across one way or another. Israel failed to keep Sabbath with God and, accordingly, would reap the consequences of it. They would be kicked out of the land for seventy years. Many wouldn't even make it to captivity, but instead died in the various raids, sieges, deportations, or attempts at escape. Despite all of this and because of the numerous promises about a coming deliverance and Deliverer,[1] God would be compassionate and gracious towards His people. Among those living in captivity in a foreign land, He would faithfully set apart a remnant and, after seventy years, lead them out.

Another Kind of Exodus

This was going to be something akin to another exodus for God's people. Isaiah 43:1-21 anticipates a day when Israel would be divinely rescued from a foreign land, much like when they were rescued from the land of Egypt, and returned to their own soil in the land of their ancestors. But, how would God do it? One thing we do know is that it wasn't going to happen the same way as before. That would be all too easy for God:

> *Do not remember the past events, pay no attention to things of old. Look, I am about to do something new; even now it is coming. Do you not see it? Indeed, I will make a way in the wilderness, rivers in the desert.* (Is 43:18-19, HCSB)

Regardless of how God was going to perform this miracle, it is obvious that He was going to do it without the help of His people. Like all of His acts of deliverance, God is the Savior, not people: "I, even I, am the LORD, and there is no savior besides Me." (Is 43:11)

Nehemiah was a cupbearer to the King of Babylon, the most powerful empire in the world in that day, not unlike Egypt was in its day. This man of Israel was broken-hearted over the news of vast ruin in his nation's capitol city, Jerusalem (Neh 1:1-3). He is so emotionally devastated by the state of his people and his homeland, he spontaneously weeps, mourns, fasts, and prays for several days (1:4). When he approaches God in prayer, the only thing he can do is call upon God's mercy. He humbly confesses the sin that consumed him and his nation (1:5-7). He remembers both the clear warnings of destruction (1:8), that Israel would have no excuse, as well as the hopeful promises of redemption (1:9-10). In doing so, Nehemiah plainly understands that neither he nor his countrymen and women have anything to offer to help the situation, that is, to bring about their own deliverance.

As the story goes, Nehemiah is miraculously granted favor on a staggering number of levels in the eyes of the Babylonian king. God works in such a way that Nehemiah is given permission by the king to return with a contingent of people to his homeland and rebuild it. If this weren't enough, Nehemiah is also given materials and resources to help him in his work, once again, not unlike how Israel left Egypt with a great deal of Egypt's resources. But there's even more: Nehemiah and those who are rebuilding are also given the king's protection. Unreal—this actually happened!

Eventually, the work gets underway and the city begins to rebuild. Along the way, the Levites give an address to the people (9:1-5a), reminding them of how they got in this position to begin with. God had built their nation from Abraham (9:5b-8). He delivered them from slavery in Egypt and protected them in the wilderness (9:9-12, 20-22). Israel "thanked" Him by ignoring His commands, including Sabbath (9:13-19). Nevertheless, God still brought them into the land promised to them (9:23-25). Israel continued to rebel against their Maker (9:26-27), even after being delivered and given rest on several occasions (9:28-35). And now, they are slaves once more in need of God's deliverance (9:36-37). The people go on to sign a covenant (9:38–10:39), promising that they will turn their hearts to honor and obey God again, including the practice of Sabbath (10:31).

. . .

The Sabbath and National Restoration

However, after some time, Israel becomes "like a dog that returns to his vomit" (Prov 26:11) and returns to the "vomit" of practices that got them into trouble in the first place. Nehemiah has to hastily and forcefully reprimand those who are dishonoring the Sabbath (13:15-22). As he recorded it,

> *Then I reprimanded the nobles of Judah and said to them, "What is this evil thing you are doing, by profaning the Sabbath day? Did not your fathers do the same, so that our God brought on us and on this city all this trouble? Yet you are adding to the wrath on Israel by profaning the Sabbath."* (13:17-18)

In some ways, it is not hard to imagine myself doing exactly what those disobedient Israelites were doing. Once again, put yourself in their shoes.

Imagine yourself in a ruined city that needs to be rebuilt and repopulated. The city's walls were back up by that point, but the city was still vulnerable to attack (7:1-4). Their numbers were small, so withstanding an attack would be near impossible. The fields still needed work and restoration from prior ravage. Homes were destroyed, so the pains of starting over are very real. This isn't exactly an ideal situation. There is a mountain of work to be done, too few hands to help, too many villains in opposition, and seemingly too little time to make the situation tenable.

In fact, the situation was so desperate that Nehemiah had to harshly rebuke the people for starting to manipulate and oppress one another for the sake of trying to establish themselves again (5:1-19). They were engaging in that ancient practice of "looking out for number one." If I'm an Israelite at that moment in time, I am mourning the fact that coffee won't be discovered for roughly another millennia because there are going to be a lot of long days and late nights, for who knows how long.

And Nehemiah wants to lecture the people for not practicing Sabbath? Really?!

However, that is exactly the point, is it not? The fact that they were once again walking the streets of Jerusalem was only because God was merciful and chose to act and complete a work on behalf of His people. And this people had nothing to contribute. Their deliverance from a land where they were effectively slaves again came about solely because of the work of their Savior. They were able to rebuild the city walls, even in the face of such discouraging opposition (2:1-20; 4:1-14; 6:1-14), solely because God was for them and with them, to help them and to fight for them (2:20; 4:20; 6:16).

Everything they experienced in this season of national restoration was a gracious gift from the hand of their God. And what better way to honor this great and generous work of God, than to pause and rest and trust by practicing Sabbath! What better way to actively remember the fact that this work, along with all of the great works of the past, was both initiated and completed by the mighty hand of God alone, without the help of human effort, than to regularly cease from labor and rest on the Sabbath?

A Holy "Reset" Button

It is clear that Sabbath was not just a command to test the faith and obedience of Israel. It was also a gift to help their hearts to be at rest. It was given as an opportunity for regular recalibration of the heart. It was a weekly restoration of perspective. In those days, there was indeed a lot of work to be done in rebuilding Jerusalem. However, it was to be done from a posture of faith and rest in the absolutely certain and completed works of their God, *not* from a posture of panic, desperation, and uncertainty.

Perhaps in those days of rebuilding, Israel remembered one of their cherished psalms from generations past, one that was traditionally sung by pilgrims during the ascent up the mountain to Jerusalem:

> *Unless the LORD builds a house, the work of the builders is wasted. Unless the LORD protects a city, guarding it with sentries will do no good. It is useless for you to work so hard from early morning until late at night, anxiously working for food to eat; for God gives rest to his loved ones.* (Ps 127:1-2, NLT)

The human race is (un-) naturally bent towards self-reliance and self-salvation. Therefore God, in His unending and unsurpassed wisdom, knew that we needed a regular reminder to rest in His sufficiency. That reminder was and is Sabbath.

Time and again, the Bible reinforces the truth that God's provision for His people is complete—past, present, and future. In the event that this would ever be in doubt, His provision would culminate and be revealed in fullest and clearest form at the advent of Jesus Christ, that is, when "the Word became flesh and dwelt among us" (Jn 1:14). In this advent, in this bodily arrival of the Son of God into this broken world, the relationship between the Sabbath and the Gospel of God's provision would be put on full display.

13

JESUS AND THE SABBATH: GOD AS SERVANT

"Jesus said to them [the Pharisees], 'The Sabbath was made for man, and not man for the Sabbath. So the Son of Man is Lord even of the Sabbath.'" (Mark 2:27-28)

A humble and unassuming manger, normally reserved for the use of animals, was presumably the first resting place of the infant Jesus, the Son of God. This is appropriate, as it powerfully symbolizes the life and ministry that was appointed for Him. Jesus had to deal with a lot of unpleasant things during His ministry on the earth. The matter of a torturous, shameful, and wholly undeserving crucifixion for sin was, of course, the worst by far, albeit the most essential. Still, I can only imagine that second place went to His dealings with people who twisted and misrepresented the words and intentions of God in order to control their surroundings and other people. Jesus had to battle with this throughout His ministry, and it largely centered on a group of people known as the Pharisees.

Their origins are under some debate. Regardless, what

they had become by the time Jesus incarnated into our world to "tread our sod"[1] was nothing short of a massive stumbling block on which a host of people tripped, fell, and were almost beyond recovery. During our family's days in Colorado, a friend of mine once pointed out to me that Jesus reserved His harshest criticisms for people like the Pharisees. Sadly, it took me several years to realize what Smokey meant by that, but I eventually understood how right he was.[2]

Jesus never held anything back, perhaps except for a just and divine wrath, when dealing with this group of spiritual leaders that were nothing more than blind guides of the blind (Mt 15:14; 23:16, 24). Right in front of His eyes, these Pharisees would even be a source of stumbling for Jesus' very own twelve disciples. Remarkably, a number of these confrontations between them took place as a result of a misunderstanding of the Sabbath.

Misrepresenting the Sabbath

On one such occasion, the disciples were following their Rabbi through fields of grain on the Sabbath day. Along the way, they were picking heads of grain in order to enjoy them as a snack on-the-go. The account indicates that the Pharisees pounced on this perceived opportunity to shame and discredit Jesus and His ministry: "Look, why are they doing what is not lawful on the Sabbath?" (Mk 2:24).

At this point in history, it seems the practice of Sabbath had jumped to the other end of the spectrum. What was previously repeated occasions of outright neglect become, instead, so constrained and rigid that its original meaning and intentions had been lost. Jesus would have to repeatedly communicate this lesson to these dreadful objects of

His faithful love. Generally speaking, the Israelites of this time period were crushed under a small mountain of extra-biblical layers of regulation concerning not only Sabbath, but also a number of other matters regarding God's Law. This happened largely at the influence of these leaders and others like them.

The response Jesus gave them was to recall a story from the Hebrew Scriptures (the Christian Old Testament), about how David broke several ceremonial laws while fleeing for his life from Saul, the Benjaminite, who was king at that time. As the story goes in 1 Samuel 21:1-10, David stopped in the city of Nob and had an exchange with Ahimelech, the priest at the time. In the course of conversation, David lies to Ahimelech by telling him that he is on a special, covert mission from the king and is headed to a meeting in another location. David then asks from Ahimelech food for himself and his men. Ahimelech apparently has nothing to offer them, except for the sacred Bread of the Presence, which was used ceremonially in worship to God.

Just in case His opponents forgot these details, Jesus would remind them of the severity of what took place:

> *Have you never read what David did, when he was in need and was hungry, he and those who were with him: how he entered the house of God, in the time of Abiathar the high priest, and ate the bread of the Presence, which it is not lawful for any but the priests to eat, and also gave it to those who were with him?* (Mk 2:25-26, ESV).[3]

In responding this way, "Jesus set forth the basic principle that human need should take precedence over ceremonial laws,"[4] something that would be an issue in Mark 3:1-5 as well, when Jesus heals the man with a withered hand on the Sabbath. Jesus was showing them that they were missing the whole point of Sabbath. Praise God that the Son of God, the holy and righteous One, entered into our ceremonially and comprehensively unclean world in order to save us from our infirmity of sin.

To further clarify what Jesus is after,

> *He claims that the Pharisees, with all their hedging restrictions, originally designed to avoid any possibility of infringing the Sabbath, had ended by making the Sabbath an intolerable burden (cf. Mt 23:4). They had by now quite forgotten that in origin the Sabbath was God's merciful provision for his creatures.*[5]

We see this most explicitly when Jesus says, "The Sabbath was made for man, and not man for the Sabbath" (Mk 2:27). To put it in plainest terms, the Sabbath was given as a gift in order to serve the needs of men and *not* in order than men may serve the (supposed) needs, demands, or requirements of the Sabbath.

Jesus, the Lord of the Sabbath

That Jesus finishes this teaching with the statement, "So the Son of Man is Lord even of the Sabbath" (Mk 2:28), would have shocked His hearers. It is vital to understanding what He is trying to communicate. Of course, part of it is the fact that He is Lord, God, Son of David, Christ, King, etc.[6] But He is also saying that, just as the title "Son of Man" belongs to Him, so does the title "Lord of the Sabbath." Jesus is the Lord and Author of this gracious gift that was given to serve the immense and unending needs of men.

When the Pharisees were misunderstanding and, consequently, abusing and destroying the purpose of the

Sabbath with their ungodly regulations, they were attacking the very nature of God. By demanding that men and women slavishly serve the (supposed) requirements surrounding the Sabbath in order to stay right with God, they were blinded and, in turn, blinding others from the very heart of Sabbath itself. When the Pharisees lived and taught Sabbath in such a way that made men and women to be servants of it, they were in fact placing the emphasis of service on the wrong person.

From the very beginning, who has been the needy one —God or humanity? From the very beginning, who has been doing the serving? From the very beginning, who has been the principal carrier of the burdens of humanity?

Jesus, the Servant of Humanity

The Bible unquestioningly portrays the God of Israel as the One who benevolently serves the needs of His creation. He is the God who patiently observes and understands the unending poverty of His creatures, and who faithfully cares and provides for them. As we have seen over and over again, it is abundantly clear that this God is the one with all the resources and ability. Although mankind has been graced with the sacred *imago Dei*, we are also beholden to God for meeting every need from His superabundant supply.

As the Apostle Paul would later preach before the crowds in Athens,

> *The God who made the world and all things in it, since He is Lord of heaven and earth, does not dwell in temples made with hands; nor is He served by human hands, as though He needed anything, since He Himself gives to all people life and breath and all things.* (Acts 17:24-25)

This God is the cosmically powerful and generous Servant of His creation. In fact, He is the prime Servant, not us. We are the ones in need of service. We are the ones in dire need of rescue, of healing, of mercy, of kindness. God Himself, in Christ, had come to do that in the most tangible way possible: in the very same flesh that we possess.

Jesus was free to (frequently) heal on the Sabbath not just because He is Lord of it, but because it was the perfect time to demonstrate and remind humanity both that we are the ones in need and that He is the *only One* who can provide for that need. Can one think of a more perfect day on which to demonstrate this reality than the Sabbath, the day when God's people were meant to rest from their labors? Only in light of this reality can any sense be made of the fact that Jesus would later permit others to do good on the Sabbath (e.g. Mt 12:9-13).[7]

Only upon this bedrock understanding of the Sabbath —that God is the true and perfect and willing Servant on our behalf—can we perform any work at all that pleases God. This is precisely why Jesus would later say that He "did not come to be served, but to serve, and to give His life a ransom for many." (Mk 10:45) He is the Servant, and we are the bankrupt objects of His service. There is no other way that God will have it because He is the God of Sabbath. It is also no wonder, then, that Jesus would make this statement to a people crushed under misguided and excessive regulation:

> *Come to Me, all of you who are weary and burdened, and I will give you rest. All of you, take up My yoke and learn from Me, because I am gentle and humble in heart, and you will find rest for yourselves. For My yoke is easy and My burden is light.* (Mt 11:28-30, HCSB)

What's even more fascinating about this statement is that it comes on the back of Jesus saying: "I praise You, Father, Lord of heaven and earth, because You have hidden these things from the wise and learned and revealed them to infants." (11:25, HCSB)

One will not find a more needy and helpless creature on planet earth than an infant. An infant simply will not survive unless someone—anyone—intervenes and provides the care that is essential to meet their many needs. An infant will not live long at all unless someone willingly takes on the mantle of a servant, even to the point of self-sacrifice, in order to overcome their helplessness. This illustration explains very well what Jesus is after here. We are all infants and God is the Caregiver. This position spits in the face of humanity's tendency towards and desire for self-reliance and self-righteousness. But God is pleased when it is this way because that is how He intended it be. This is the way that highlights the beauty of the Gospel.

By abusing the Sabbath, we foolishly fall back into old trappings of unbelief and sin, with perhaps the worst of these being the lie that we need be the servants of God in order to gain His pleasure. This attitude is woefully offensive to God because, in doing so, we are robbing God of His joyful desire to be the self-sacrificing Servant on our behalf, and we are also calling His service to us unnecessary. This is a harrowing thought, and the absolute antithesis of the Gospel.

14

JESUS AND THE SABBATH: GOD AS HEALER

"And He [Jesus] said to them, 'What man is there among you who has a sheep, and if it falls into a pit on the Sabbath, will he not take hold of it and lift it out? How much more valuable then is a man than a sheep! So then, it is lawful to do good on the Sabbath.' Then He said to the man, 'Stretch out your hand!' He stretched it out, and it was restored to normal, like the other. But the Pharisees went out and conspired against Him, as to how they might destroy Him." (Matthew 12:11-14)

Although I still have so much to learn about people and why we do the things we do, I am already quite convinced of our comprehensively foolish conceit. We claim to have the answer for the world's complicated, ages-long problems and, meanwhile, freely and confidently judge and slander those who give even a hint of disagreement. All the while, our weakness is so glaring it is absurd.[1] It is no wonder Jesus used the speck-and-plank illustration in His teachings (Mt 7:1-5), because to actually see such a thing in real life would have been ridiculous—comedic even. These thoughts bring my mind to the matter of sickness.

Sickness, a Great Humiliator

The very nature of sickness is such a powerful thing. There have been times, often when doubled-over in pain or shaking from a fever, that I have found myself contemplating the power of sickness and what it can teach us. We are regularly brought to our knees by tiny, microscopic organisms. One day, a man or woman in a position of great power could be arrogantly boasting from their lips in a boardroom meeting, and the next day be violently heaving from those same lips over a disgusting toilet. In fact, now that I think about it, this is the perfect image for our true condition.

We are so confident in our own strength and our own resiliency one day and then doubled-over in agonizing weakness the next. And, in those moments of great human limitation, we are left embracing the sides of a vessel that was made to catch human waste as if it were our best friend, and allowing its porcelain touch to soothe our discomfort as if it were "as cool as the other side of the pillow."[2] For some of us, even, it is those stomach twisting, brain-pounding, or radiology room moments that we perhaps call upon God for the first time in who knows how long. Certainly, if death is the great equalizer, then sickness must be a close second.

Jim Gaffigan, known internationally for his various comedy outlets, when writing about the panic of losing a child in a New York City park, also commented on the phenomenon that is the power of sickness to get people's attention in matters of faith:

"Hey, God, I know I haven't talked to you in a while. . . . Anyway, if you can help me find my son, I promise I will never do anything bad again. I won't even eat at Wendy's—oh, wait. There he is. Never mind, God. Well, we're off to Wendy's. Talk to you when I get cancer." Kids and disease are the true gateways to faith.[3]

At its basest level, sickness reminds us of our inherent and pervasive weakness and neediness.

Sure there are some diseases that are curable, and let's all take a moment to genuinely thank God for that gift, but not all the corresponding medicines are universally available to all people in all places. Outside of those treatable conditions, there are numerous ones that we have no clue how to address or slow down. This is a painful reminder that, as awful as sickness can be, that isn't even the scariest part. If the sickness is bad enough, we are ultimately reminded of our mortality.

Certain types of cancer have been wreaking havoc on families for generations. As of the original writing of these words, there is still no cure for acquired immunodeficiency syndrome (AIDS). With regularity, the news reminds of us some new strain of flu that is killing a host of people in some part of the world. There are also orthopedic issues, where a patient may be treated for years yet still never experience alleviation from pain or a full recovery to what would be considered normal. The list of sicknesses goes on and on. And let's not forget the egregious evils of biological warfare—*Can you believe it? We actually manufacture illness for personal gain!*—with people making money, hand over fist, by creating sicknesses that are deadlier than ever.

Now imagine what I just described, but two millennia ago. Imagine dealing with the suffering of sickness without the vast number of medicinal breakthroughs that have been achieved. Imagine the hopelessness of draining your family's entire savings on treating something that can be covered by a copay today.[4] Imagine the chronic pain of a hunched-back that won't go away, or the social stigma of being a leper who is not only dramatically avoided by others, but also unable to worship corporately because of ritual uncleanness. Or, similarly, imagine having to endure years-long embarrassment, inconvenience, and frustration of having an unceasing feminine flow of blood. Imagine having a fever that could lead to death, or having a hand that is withered to the point of (presumably) hindering one's ability to engage in a trade and earn a living. This is the world into which Jesus entered, into which He came as Servant and as Healer. And, thankfully, He was willing to perform some of His work on the Sabbath.

Jesus, the Compassionate Healer

One Sabbath day—more than likely, it is the same day on which the Pharisees were corrected in the fields of grain—Jesus entered the synagogue and encountered a man with a withered hand. Yet again, He was met with opposition by a brand of religious fervor that was not in accordance with knowledge, as would later be described in Rom 10:1-4. Blinded by this ignorant zeal, the Pharisees proceed to ask Jesus whether or not it was lawful to heal on the Sabbath (Mt 12:10). It may seem like a crazy question to many of us today[5] but, again, this is the world into which Jesus entered.

The Divine Servant-Healer responds by explaining that anyone who has or possesses a sheep that falls into a pit on the Sabbath, will certainly go and rescue it (12:11). That being the case, how much more important is it that a man be rescued (i.e. healed) on the Sabbath (12:12), especially when one remembers that a person is made in the image of God? Jesus then proceeds to heal the man and fully restore his hand (12:13).

Similarly to the prior chapter, we are reminded about the heart of the Sabbath, and ultimately the Gospel, through the demonstration of God's great provision in the face of humanity's great need. The Sabbath should have been a weekly reminder of this ever-present reality of life and of relating to God. Instead, it became an opportunity in the eyes of some to demonstrate their personal ability, resiliency, and adequacy by adhering to a rigid (but incorrect) understanding of the Sabbath.

This healing, among others, was meant to be a reminder that the God of Israel is so compassionate and gentle towards our obvious and all-consuming infirmity, that He was not even willing to extinguish a dimly burning candle or break a badly bruised reed (12:17-21; cf. Is 42:1-3). This is what the Sabbath was to expresses but, instead, it became a platform for the "strong" to trample on the "weak." Or, in other words, it became an opportunity for some of us to demonstrate how well we can serve God, even if others can't keep up, instead of it being a reminder that God is the One who has served us, chiefly in the Gospel, because He knew we couldn't "keep up" with Him —in every sense, including righteousness.

Jesus, the Friend of Sinners

This whole scene is very reminiscent of an occasion when Jesus addresses the Pharisees over the matter of spending time with sinners. And, appropriate to the topic at hand, Jesus responds by way of a mini-parable:

Then it happened that as Jesus was reclining at the table in the house, behold, many tax collectors and sinners came and were dining with Jesus and His disciples. When the Pharisees saw this, they said to His disciples, "Why is your Teacher eating with the tax collectors and sinners?" But when Jesus heard this, He said, "It is not those who are healthy who need a physician, but those who are sick. But go and learn what this means: 'I DESIRE COMPASSION, AND NOT SACRIFICE,' for I did not come to call the righteous, but sinners." (Mt 9:10-13)

This perfectly illustrates the point that Jesus is trying to make. He is the God of the Sabbath, the day that was to remind us of our great need and God's great, perfect, and complete provision. The Pharisees saw in themselves such ability and sufficiency that they considered it possible to keep the Law. Therefore, they were offended that this so-called Messiah would spend time with sinners, those who failed repeatedly at keeping the Law.

They were completely blind to their own need, and Jesus saw right through it. Naturally, therefore, He likened their situation to a Healer who is only willing and able to heal those who acknowledge their sickness. This is both literal and figurative. A doctor cannot care for or heal someone who does not see the need to visit him or her. Similarly, matters of sin and human frailty require a willingness to admit that something is wrong and that it won't go away on its own, without some outside help. This would be the perfect opportunity for Jesus to "drop the mic," so to speak. However, being so amazing in His wisdom and understanding, Jesus adds to this: "Now go and learn the meaning of this Scripture: 'I want you to show mercy, not offer sacrifices.'" (9:13, NLT).

God Marries a Whore

Jesus finished this epic teaching with a reference to something the Pharisees had likely committed to memory, or at the very least read on several occasions by that point in their lives. He very appropriately points them to Hosea 6:6, which was written by a prophet who was commanded by God to do something rather difficult and, let's just say it, unbelievably scandalous. Hosea was going to be a living parable before the people of Israel by marrying a prostitute whom God said ahead of time would be unfaithful to him. If you've never read the book of Hosea, you need to. It is tragic, beautiful, and humbling.[6]

Near the middle of the book, God gives Hosea some words that he is to relate to the people. Hosea, warning the people again and again (and again) to repent of sin, calls his countrymen to return to their God (6:1:1-3). Although the people are torn, their God will heal them (6:1a). Although wounded, He will bandage them (6:2b). Though they are dead, He will raise them up (6:2). God's promise to visit His people is so certain, it will be like the daily coming of dawn (6:3a). And His visitation will be so refreshing, it will be like rain upon the earth (6:3b). God's people are so indescribably unfaithful (6:4), He had to bring ruin to them in order to remind them of their helplessness (6:5). They are like Adam who *transgressed the covenant* and dealt treacherously with their God (6:7). However, in the swamp of their ruin is an opportunity to remember that their sole task is *not* serving God (i.e. sacrifice and burnt offerings) but rather knowing and loving Him (i.e. loyalty and knowledge).

The connection between this portion of Hosea, how Jesus uses it, and what we have discovered about Sabbath is staggering, all the way down to the reference back to where it all started—with Adam (and Eve)! Once again, it is God's great kindness that led Him to give the gift of

Sabbath for His people to regularly recalibrate the posture and orientation of their hearts.

Many have experienced how quickly and easily one can get lost in misdirected religious exercise, to the point where love for God evaporates. We are so prone to get caught up in the checklist of what we assume should get done in order for God to be pleased with us, that we completely overlook the simple (but profound) reality that God has chosen to relate to us at all. If we are willing to be honest with ourselves about who we *really* are, then any indication that God still chooses to love us should instantly ignite our hearts into a wildfire of affection for our Creator and Savior. It would burn and rage so hotly that no amount self-righteous "service" could quench it. And yet, this is not our reality, is it? We are constantly needy, both for reminders of God's mercy and of God's service towards us.

Regarding this chapter's topic of healing, I fully believe that God still supernaturally heals people without the use of medical intervention. Without robbing from this statement at all, I also believe He graciously and generously heals by way of medical skill and knowledge. And this only highlights the point we're making even more. With all of these amazing medical gifts from God, are we not still in great need and still incredibly vulnerable? Additionally, those diseases or situations where one's only hope is a literal miracle serve as another essential reminder. That is, despite all of our advancements and all of history's cumulative human innovation, we are still dreadfully poor and sick and needy, unable to deliver ourselves, and still very much in need of God's able and healing hand.

Therefore, sickness is indeed an opportunity to remind us of our need for Sabbath.

15

JESUS AND THE SABBATH: GOD
AS LIGHT

*"Then Jesus again spoke to them [the scribes and the
Pharisees], saying, 'I am the Light of the world; he who
follows Me will not walk in the darkness, but will have the
Light of life.' . . . Therefore they picked up stones to throw at
Him, but Jesus hid Himself and went out of the temple. As
He passed by, He saw a man blind from birth. And His
disciples asked Him, 'Rabbi, who sinned, this man or his
parents, that he would be born blind?' Jesus answered, 'It
was neither that this man sinned, nor his parents; but it was
so that the works of God might be displayed in him . .
. While I am in the world, I am the Light of the
world.' When He had said this, He spat on the ground, and
made clay of the spittle, and applied the clay to his eyes, and
said to him, 'Go, wash in the pool of Siloam' (which is
translated, Sent). So he went away and washed, and came
back seeing."* (John 8:12, 59; 9:1-7)

The Gospel account of John contains a long section of
Sabbath speech, starting in chapter eight through
the midway point of chapter ten. It begins in the early

morning, when Jesus enters the temple and is confronted by His opponents with a woman caught in adultery. Naturally, Jesus shuts the mouths of His opponents (temporarily) with some pretty compelling teaching about one's attitude towards sin, both in ourselves and in others (8:1-11). Then, Jesus calls Himself "the Light of the world," after which He launches into several confrontational teachings about a number of topics (8:12-58). At the conclusion of this long teaching in chapter eight, the people are so upset that they are preparing to stone Him. However, Jesus leaves the temple before that can happen (8:59). On His way, He passes a blind man. How appropriate and, as we will soon see, how timely as well!

The account goes like this: Jesus and the disciples encounter the blind man, a situation which raises a theological problem (9:1-2). The man is blind, so somebody must be at fault; somebody sinned. Jesus negates this possibility immediately, saying that the man's birth into blindness is part of God's plan for God's glory (9:3). Then, Jesus calls Himself "the Light of the world" again and heals the man (9:4-7). Naturally, this causes a bit of a stir among the crowds, since everyone knew that this man was born blind, but now his sight has been fully restored (9:8-12). The stir turns into a full-on commotion once Jesus' religious opponents get word of it (9:13). The man gets questioned thoroughly by the Pharisees, as do the man's parents, because they cannot believe it at all possible that Jesus could heal the man (9:15-23). After all, as they put it, "This man is not from God, for he does not keep the Sabbath. . . How can a man who is a sinner do such signs?" (9:16, ESV) Enraged, the religious leaders question the man again once more and, in the end, verbally shame him and throw him out (9:24-34).

The scene continues when the man again encounters

Jesus, who calls him to believe in the Son of Man. He adds, "For judgment I came into this world, that those who do not see may see, and those who see may become blind." (9:39, ESV) This is followed by more teaching, namely that Jesus is the Good Shepherd who lays His life down for His sheep (10:1-18), with the scene at last closing on great division among the Jewish people over Him (10:19-21). Again, in case you missed, this all happened on the same day: the Sabbath (9:13-16).

The Power of Darkness

Darkness is a very powerful image not only in the Bible, but also in cultures and literature and art worldwide. Both film and stage have routinely used dark elements to visually portray or hint at one character being bad or villainous. Darkness has also been used to bring a heightened sense of suspense and even terror. If many scenes that are cast in darkness, instead, took place in a setting of light, then it would be considerably less effective at evoking fear. The imagery of darkness is well-known to us.

At the risk of turning the stomachs of some readers, one of the most critically acclaimed examples of this is found in the film, *The Silence of the Lambs*.[1] Without going into the various grotesque details—and the reader has been warned that they are indeed sickening at times—the climax of the film finds the heroine unexpectedly trapped in a dark house with (one of) the film's villains. It is approximately three minutes of cinematic cardiac arrest. One of the chief reasons for this is due to the main character's momentary debilitation in pitch darkness, unable to see anything, while the antagonist ominously creeps towards her in night-vision goggles. Another example of a similar use of darkness in film is found in the Audrey Hepburn classic thriller, *Wait Until Dark*.[2] At the film's apex, there is a significant confrontation that is notoriously distressing, primarily due to the fact that the heroine's experience of darkness is complete because she is blind. Viewers can see everything, but the scenes are fraught with tension because they know that the main character is completely "in the dark," as it were. The presence of a consuming darkness does nothing but amplify the vulnerability of the situation.

Children throughout human history, and even adults at times, have been scared of the dark at one point or another. No matter how often we are reminded that there are no monsters under the bed; that there are no ghosts in the closet; that someone is not in another part of the house; that the noise heard was just the cat freaking out in the other room; that all of the razor-sharp LEGO® bricks really were cleaned-up from off of the floor[3]—it doesn't matter. The dark still makes us edgy. We can't see everything. We don't *really* know what's there. We are in the dark. And it scares us.

The Darkness of Sin

The Bible is not afraid to use darkness as a teaching point. From the very beginning, when the world is without form and void, it is also described as dark (Gen 1:2) until God says, "Let there be light" (1:3). The first thing God does is turn on the light. Darkness is used to describe distressing sleep (Gen 15:12); ominous eclipse events (Ex 10:21-22); the dread of an infinitely holy God at Mt. Sinai (Deut 4:11); the terrifying fate of those who refuse to repent of evil (1 Sam 2:9); personal depression (Ps 18:28); spiritual blindness (Ps 82:5; Prov 2:12-13; Ecc 2:13-14); the oppression of prison (Is 42:7); the judgment of God (Joel 2:1-2); and so on. Quite notably, it is even present at the crucifixion of Jesus, casting both a literal and proverbial shadow over the whole scene.

Perhaps most repeatedly and forcefully, darkness is used to describe the state of humanity in our sin, apart from the light of God or the God of light—either phrase works. Not only are we spiritually blind people, unable to see and groping around in our own personal darkness, but we are also surrounded by the general darkness of this world and in those around us. Darkness is also used to describe the unseen, but still very real, spiritual forces that are at work in this world in opposition to God and His people. All of that darkness and more is certain to persist for the whole of humanity in this life and on into eternity unless something is done about it.

We might consider saving ourselves, but Jesus says this is as likely to succeed as a blind person giving themselves the gift of sight. Or, similarly, maybe we deem ourselves capable enough to lead others to truth. To that, Jesus once said, "Every plant not planted by my heavenly Father will be uprooted, so ignore them. They are blind guides leading the blind, and if one blind person guides another, they will both fall into a ditch." (Mt 15:13-14, NLT) Or, further still, perhaps we estimate the abilities of humanity as sufficient enough to push back the darkness of evil, somewhat like one person turns on the light for another in a dark room. However, if we soberly consider the scope and history of the ills of humanity, that's a pretty presumptuous reach, to say the least. Our failures to comprehensively right the wrongs of this world stretch on *ad infinitum*.

This is why Jesus unreservedly declares Himself as "the Light of the world." And this is also why the Old Testament provided readers with abundant prophecy, centuries before Jesus came, about God bringing light (Himself) into our darkness. While the examples are really quite numerous, let's look at just a few.

The Light of Jesus

I have heard Isaiah 9:1-2 quoted around Christmas time because of how it is used in Matthew 4:15-16, with Jesus being the bringer of light into darkness. The Gospel writer, John, likes to use the imagery of light in a good vs. evil kind of way to show how Jesus is the all-consuming Light in the midst of our darkness (1:4-5; 3:16-21; 8:12; 9:5; 12:35-36; etc). In Jesus' own words, "I have come into the world as light, so that whoever believes in me may not remain in darkness." (Jn 12:46, ESV)

In the Sabbath day scene of John 8-10, this imagery of God's light invading our darkness is on full display. The arrogance of man is confronted by the truth of Jesus, who mercifully deals with us, even though we are utterly blind to how lost we really are. His opponents (all of us) get angry with Him when He chooses to point out that we are sinful, trapped in a cold and hopeless darkness, and in desperate need of God's warming and illuminating radiance. We are furious at the thought that anyone would dare to call into question our ability and intelligence and wisdom; that one would be audacious enough to say we are actually blind, and insist that we are constantly on the precipice of our own demise, groping in the dark, and in desperate need for someone else to open our eyes.

This is why, in this particular healing, Jesus opened the eyes of a blind man on the Sabbath and bookended that miraculous encounter with an emphatic, "I am the light of the world." That this took place on the Sabbath day reminds us of the heart of the Sabbath and the Gospel. It provides a perfect opportunity to remember the desperation of our darkness, the despair of our blindness, and the absolutely essential and sufficient provision of God to bring His light and open our eyes. Jesus was pleased to turn on the light then, as He also was in the very beginning; so He also is now.

16

JESUS AND THE SABBATH: GOD AS SAVIOR

"Now he was teaching in one of the synagogues on the Sabbath. And there was a woman who had had a disabling spirit for eighteen years. She was bent over and could not fully straighten herself. When Jesus saw her, he called her over and said to her, 'Woman, you are freed from your disability.' And he laid his hands on her, and immediately she was made straight, and she glorified God. But the ruler of the synagogue, indignant because Jesus had healed on the Sabbath, said to the people, 'There are six days in which work ought to be done. Come on those days and be healed, and not on the Sabbath day.' Then the Lord answered him, 'You hypocrites! Does not each of you on the Sabbath untie his ox or his donkey from the manger and lead it away to water it? And ought not this woman, a daughter of Abraham whom Satan bound for eighteen years, be loosed from this bond on the Sabbath day?'" (Luke 13:10-16, ESV)

One day, all of the evils of the world will be eliminated and the redeemed people of God will live in His presence for all eternity. This is a work that God will do in fullest measure, without our help.[1] In the mean time, people may and should labor to see the freedom of God's kingdom expressed here and now, even if it be limited in scope or duration. Any glimpse of freedom in this world is meant to be a cause for hope in the world that is to come. Nevertheless, as striking as they are, these glimpses will only remain as such: mere glimpses. These victories will be only shadows reflecting what will be one day when God brings about the substance. Until that day comes, the horrors of our evil in this world provide us pictures or illustrations of how God works. Take, for example, the matter of slavery.

Enslaved to Sin

There are numerous examples of the atrocities of slavery throughout human history. This includes expressions of it in American history, as well as millennia before, in the days of the early church and even before then. God has chosen to use it throughout redemptive history to provide a tangible example of what He does on behalf of His people. In this, God rescues His people from slavery, whether from a literal slavery in Egypt, or a figurative (but still real) slavery to sin. In either case, the point is that people are in a helpless state of slavery, and that they need to be rescued from it.

The letter of Paul to the Romans provides a powerful explanation of this. The general idea of Rom 6:16-23 is that slaves are subject to their masters and, therefore, must obey them. They have no choice in the matter. That is simply how slavery works. In this way, people are slaves to sin, bound to obey the master of sin without exception. The only way for such a situation to change is to be freed to serve a new master. In matters of sin, Jesus Christ has provided that freedom, which is why Paul urges the church in Rome to remember their freedom. In doing so, they will lovingly and joyfully give themselves to serve Jesus and righteousness. Otherwise, they will find themselves trying to return to the old master of sin.

The point is that a slave has no choice but to serve his or her master. The slave will do what the master says, whether that master be sin or Jesus. And, there can be no change in the situation unless someone outside of the slave acts. The slave cannot free him or herself.

Imprisoned in Sin

Somewhat similar to this is the example of being a prisoner. Whether rightly or wrongly practiced, and there are plenty of examples of both, the issue of incarceration can provide an insightful glimpse into how the Gospel works in our lives. A person in prison is constrained in various forms. There is often a standard-issue prison garment. There are assigned times for meals, for showers, for recreation, for just about any activity under the sun. And prisoners largely don't get to choose when to do those things. Even if there are options at some point, those options exist within a much larger system built on constraint. The former freedoms of the "outside world" have been removed, and all that remains is what is determined by someone else. In a big picture sense, any perceived freedom is merely an illusion.

The same Paul who used slavery as an example to express the Gospel did the same with prison. As one who personally experienced prison on a number of occasions, and before his conversion had others thrown in prison for following Jesus, Paul had a lot of authority to speak on the subject. He wrote extensively about how Christ both freed him from the prison or captivity of sin and the Law (Rom 7:6, 23; Gal 3:22-23), as well as made Him a prisoner to Himself (Php 1:13; 2 Tim 1:8; Phm 1:1, 9). Those who are in prison to sin and to the requirements of religious law are constrained by them and unable to operate outside their "walls". Any so-called "freedom" within these restraints is just an illusion. However, Jesus came to set us free from that destructive prison and, continuing the metaphor, make us prisoners to Himself—to His love, to His grace, to His will, and so on.

Bound by Satan

This matters because Jesus once went out of His way to "loose from bonds" a woman who had been "bound by Satan" for eighteen years. And this He did on the Sabbath. Now, I'm not going to say one way or another about what is behind the diseases in this world. Whether Satan and his demons are behind every bodily affliction, or whether it is simply the result of a fallen world, or some combination of both, I don't know. However, in *this* case, Jesus Himself makes it perfectly clear that there is a direct link between the disease and Satan.

The scene of Luke 13:10-16 presents readers with a woman that was disabled in such a way that she could not stand up straight. It wasn't that she did not want to; she simply couldn't. No matter how much she wanted to or how hard she tried to, she was relegated to being hunched over. And this was the world she lived in for eighteen years.

If you've ever done any manual labor that requires bending over a lot, you learn pretty quickly the toll that it takes on your back. Aside from the times I've helped others move, our family has moved so many times that it feels like we are modern day nomads. I cannot recall how many times I have packed, unpacked, and repacked our household goods. Then there's always the matter of loading and unloading the van, trailer, or moving truck. No matter how often I've told myself, "Lift with your legs and not your back," I seem to always finish each moving experience with some overly-sore muscles in my back because I've been bending over. And that's with me having a choice whether to not to lift heavy items in this way.

It is very, very difficult for me to imagine what it would be like to live and operate in that state for eighteen years. The difficulties that would accompany this posture would be extensive simply because the body was not meant to operate that way. Soreness and medical issues with this woman's back would eventually become soreness and medical issues in other places as well, especially considering the spine's role in human physiology. To say that she was suffering would likely not even begin to describe this woman's condition. Sure the physical toll would be tremendous, but so would the emotional toll.

After all, imagine the affect this would have on these simple but deeply-human activities: household chores, physical intimacy with one's spouse, playing with one's children, holding a friend's newborn baby, putting on nice clothing, or giving a dear friend a hug in the midst of their grief. Envision standing-out everywhere you go because of your disability: the second and third glances, or the outright staring; the hurtful gossip; the patronizing expressions of pity; and the constant well-meaning offers of help, when all you really want to do is be able to perform everyday tasks on your own.

Just about every single form of human activity and interaction would be negatively affected by this debilitating condition. And this poor woman lived with this for eighteen years. To add insult to injury, it becomes clear along the way that this woman's religious leaders were more concerned with her adherence to strict religious rigor than with her general well-being. True compassion and, presumably, intercession were afterthoughts when compared to her ability to keep the religious law in the way they thought it should be kept. Even worse, based on the words of Jesus, animals were more probable than her to receive their compassion.

The gospel writer, Luke, reinforces the lesson with a similar account in 14:1-6. Jesus visited the house of a ruler among the Pharisees, where they were to eat some bread on the Sabbath day. The bread would have been prepared the day before, so as not to violate the Sabbath, and would have served to relieve from hunger. In their presence was a man with dropsy or edema, which is a condition that causes swelling and can be seriously painful. Jesus asks them a Sabbath question, heals the man, and then uses this situation to teach them: "Which of you, having a son or an ox that has fallen into a well on a Sabbath day, will not immediately pull him out?" (14:5, ESV) He uses an example of an animal's need for rescue, even if on the Sabbath, to point out how appropriate it is for an image-bearer of God to experience an even greater rescue.

Dear reader, there may not be steel shackles and chains, and there aren't any cell bars that we can see in this scene. But, in a very real way, the woman of Luke 13 and the man of Luke 14 were without a doubt slaves and held captive as prisoners. This is why Jesus set them free. And, further, this is why He set them free on the Sabbath.

Freed by Jesus

As previously stated, Jesus Himself linked this woman's condition to the oppressive works of His enemy, Satan. She was bent over because Satan was behind it. In some way that was unseen, Satan's real power in this world was manifesting itself physically in this woman's life and making her a prisoner in her own body. Since it had been eighteen years, it is pretty obvious that all other outlets of healing were no help at all. So, she was debilitated and without hope of freedom—that is, until Jesus came along.

This woman's physical healing by the Son of God on the Sabbath is a perfect picture of the Gospel. Humanity is enslaved and imprisoned, without hope of liberation. Like a slave or a prisoner bound in chains, our only choice was to obey the limits of our sinful and self-centered restraints. But God did what neither man nor woman could do, in sending His Son to rescue us from sin and its effects, whether short-term or eternal. Jesus Christ is the Rescuer of a shackled humanity.

Sure, this can certainly have bearing on the physical consequences of sin. But it is so much more than that. It means that, by the Gospel and the indwelling Holy Spirit, God has freed us from a destiny of an absolute, hopeless imprisonment; the ultimate threats of sin, death and hell, have been defeated and we are liberated! We can have hope for a future beyond our sins and our failures. The destructive consequences of our choices, driven by fear or pride or selfishness or any other weakness we are prone to, no longer have to rule or define us. Better yet, those things no longer have to rule us in general. The Gospel gives us the ability to be courageous, humble, and others-centered. The freeing power of the Gospel can liberate us from our addictions—workaholism, substance abuse, pornography, greed, people pleasing, food, and so on. It can provide course correction and safe harbor for our thought life, our emotional health, and other intangible facets of our humanity.

Martin Luther was made famous in 1517 for posting "A Disputation on the Power and Efficacy of Indulgences," otherwise known as his "Ninety-Five Theses," on the doors of the Castle Church in Wittenberg which, alongside a number of other things, helped to launch of the Protestant Reformation. One of his more notable subsequent publications was *The Bondage of the Will*, wherein Luther contended with Erasmus, a classical humanist, over the matter of humanity's bondage to either Satan or to God:

> *Thus the human will is, as it were, a beast between the two. If God sit thereon, it wills and goes where God will . . . If Satan sit thereon, it wills and goes as Satan will. Nor is it in the power of its own will to choose, to which rider it will run, nor which it will seek; but the riders themselves contend, which shall have and hold it.* [2]

The Gospel of God's salvation is the power for freeing us *from* the bondage of Satan and for freeing us *towards* the "bondage" of life and rest in Jesus Christ. He is our eternal Rescuer, the very reason why we can be liberated from sin and, in some cases, should He choose to do so, from even our physical afflictions. And through the regular practice of Sabbath, we remember these things and we remember our freedom and our rest in Him.

17

JESUS AND THE SABBATH: GOD AS SACRIFICE

"Therefore when Jesus had received the sour wine, He said, 'It is finished!' And He bowed His head and gave up His spirit. Then the Jews, because it was the day of preparation, so that the bodies would not remain on the cross on the Sabbath (for that Sabbath was a high day), asked Pilate that their legs might be broken, and that they might be taken away. So the soldiers came, and broke the legs of the first man and of the other who was crucified with Him; but coming to Jesus, when they saw that He was already dead. . . ." (John 19:30-33)

This story of God's work for our rest reaches a watershed moment on a Roman cross, where all of the lessons collide. The crucifixion of Jesus, the Son of God, represents God's ultimate purpose in His service for us. He really did serve and heal and free people—tangibly, in the flesh and in real-time. These were tremendously benevolent things for Him to do. I still become lost in thought at times when I consider that Jesus chose to physically touch lepers when no one else would. It is incredible! Truly, there is no God like Him.

But, as great as all of this was, to stop there would be a disaster on so many levels. To leave out the work of Jesus on the cross is an egregious and damnable offense against the greatest act of service that God would ever perform on our behalf, in order to address the fallen human condition. If it helps, remember that sin is the reason why the world is fallen in the first place, why things like sickness and death are even part of the equation. Thus, all of Jesus' miraculous works ultimately point to the predetermined plan of God to send His Son into the world to deal with our sin once and for all (Acts 2:22-24).

We Are Religious (and Self-Righteous)

All over the world and throughout the ages, people and cultures and civilizations have put into place endless systems by which we can: (1) promote some kind of morality for the (assumed) greater good, (2) restrain those who might want to transgress that code, and (3) personally measure our performance in light of it. It is for this reason that I readily say that "everyone is religious," even if they claim not to be. Sure, there are broad, formalized categorizations of religion, but there are also an unlimited number of micro-religions—if you'll permit me to use the term—that are exercised throughout the world and within the heart of every individual on planet earth, without exception.

A person who believes the combination of: origins by way of "Big Bang" and macro-evolutionary processes, no existence of God, and an acceptable standard of human conduct by which people are measured as either 'good' or 'bad'—this person is a follower of that particular brand of "religion." This is the reason that you can ask most people if they consider themselves a "good person," to which almost all (in my experience) will say "yes." They are measuring themselves by some code, whether known or unknown, and want the satisfaction of knowing they are indeed "good" or, conversely, are shaken at the mere thought that they might actually be a bad person. This is where the phrase "self-righteous" truly finds it origins. If anyone believes that he or she can be *righteous* through their own personal effort and ability, then that person is *self*-righteous. Whether or not it exists under the umbrella of a known religion is irrelevant. In the end, all self-righteousness is the same.

To explain, we will follow this thread a little further. Most people you meet are eager to regard themselves as "good" because it ultimately means that they deserve a reward of some kind for living a life worthy of that designation. For those who believe in a god (or many gods), perhaps heaven is a reward for their good living. For others, perhaps it is reincarnation to a better state in the next life. For some, it may be a positive and lasting legacy that outlives them. Maybe the reward is simply ceasing to exist after death, that is, the absence or avoidance of negative consequences in the afterlife. In one way or another, every person in human history has: developed some personal, moral code (either intentionally or unintentionally); sought to live according to it; measured themselves against it; and expected some kind of reward, whether in this life or the next or whatever.

Further and interestingly, when surveying the landscape of our countless moral codes, there are really a lot of similarities. For example, the unjust or unlawful taking of a life, which we would call "murder," is in every culture around the world either against the law or, otherwise, a cause for unparalleled personal offense. Even in so-called uncivilized societies, where perhaps there is no official legal system in place, there can still be present a pattern of revenge that escalates quickly and perpetuates for multiple generations. This would not happen unless there was an inherent offensiveness to the initial action, which in turn necessitates some kind of justice or retribution.

I'm developing this thought in order to highlight the fact that our *desire for* a moral compass is universal—onboard "programming" from God. We are naturally bent to think in this way, and we cannot escape it. And, if we are willing to be honest with ourselves for even a moment, we are not able to follow these moral codes very well. Even if we are the creators of our own code or law, we still step out-of-line every now and again or, let's be honest, *all the time*. We have all transgressed our codes, especially when it has required from us the death of our convenience, our comfort, or our lofty self-perception.

I Am a Great Sinner

This is why the Bible says that the people of Israel (the Jews) were unable to keep the Law given to them by God and, similarly, why the Gentiles (non-Jews), who were *not* given a Law from God in the way that the Jews were, are nevertheless unable to keep the laws that they inevitably create for themselves (Rom 2:14-16). People are universally rule-makers and rule-breakers. We are simultaneously creators of and failures at religion.

Since we are sinners, then our greatest need is "healing" from our sins (i.e. forgiveness). This need is so great that it stretches beyond our need for physical healing, relief from difficult circumstances, or even provision of basic needs (e.g. food, water, and clothing). This need is so far-reaching that our most basic programming has been jumbled and we are broken, no longer able to function properly. We were meant to choose what is good, but we instead choose what is wrong. The Bible calls this sin because we have *missed the mark* on a cosmic target of morality.

No . . . I take that back. The issue is actually much, much deeper than just morality.

Imagine you are a parent who has worked tirelessly to care for the needs of your children. You have laid down your life for the sake of their good, so that they might grow and thrive and be all they were meant to be. You have been patient, loving, caring, kind, and overall self-sacrificing on an untold number of levels. You love your child so much, you are like a momma bear that would do some chilling and irreparable damage to anyone who might try to get in the way of the general welfare of your cub.

Now, take all of this imagery, and imagine what it would be like if your child always called someone else "mommy" or "daddy." Someone else always gets their affection, gets their smiles, gets their laughter, and gets their joy. They run to someone else for hugs and comfort when they are sad. Every outpouring of your love and devotion and care is met with a blind, ignorant, and even willful turning of your child to another's arms. If this happened to you, to call it *heartbreaking* would be a ludicrous understatement. It would be more accurate to say that, inside you, there would be an untamed, raging tempest of hurt and anger and confusion and pain unlike any other on earth. No words would be able to describe the level of offense this would cause you. There would be no wound to compare.

This is only a miniscule fraction of what it must be like for God when he sees us.

The God of the universe breathed His life into us; gave us His image; gave us intelligence; provided for us; gave us friendships, marriage, and sex; gave us amazing sensory-related gifts like music, taste buds, and mountains; and so much more. This God did all of this and indescribably more; yet we ignore Him and wildly give our hearts and affections to an endless list of other things. It is simply unbelievable. Sin goes dramatically beyond a simple breaking of the rules. We have literally disgraced our very essence, the *imago Dei*; transgressed our essential purpose, dragging God's beautiful name and character through the mud; cheated and robbed one another into an unjust and miserable oblivion; narcissistically marveled at our perceived greatness; and, in all of it, foolishly urged others to do the same. Humanity has done all of this in an endless cycle of self-congratulating self-destruction. To say that we have offended God is to put words to something on a level of evil that there is simply no words for.

The Punishment Fits the Crime

When one thinks about punishment or retribution, we must remember it is measured not only by the offense itself, but also by the person against whom the offense takes place. To provide a very basic example, if I were to steal my neighbor's wallet, I would likely either pay some relatively smaller fine or go to jail for some relatively small period of time. On the other hand, if I were to murder my neighbor, I would go to jail for a long time, possibly even for life. Depending on the jurisdiction in which I am tried, I could possibly be executed. The weight of the offense determines the weight of the punishment.

Now, imagine those same scenarios, but that they were instead committed against a less obscure figure. Imagine the justice brought to a person who was caught stealing the wallet of the CEO of a Fortune 500 company. Or, to go even further, imagine the awful scenario of one making an attempt on the life of the President of the United States or the sheik of a Middle Eastern nation. The degree of swiftness and the level of retribution against such a crime would be frightening. If the perpetrator was not instantly obliterated, or at the very least hospitalized, by the Secret Service agents or personal bodyguards sworn to protect him or her, the offender would no doubt be tried in the highest court for the highest possible conviction.

If we translate this line of thinking now to a cosmically holy God, our Maker and Provider, we shudder in terror at what we deserve. Perhaps it is best to let Scripture speak for itself at this point:

> *Anyone who has set aside the Law of Moses dies without mercy on the testimony of two or three witnesses. How much severer punishment do you think he will deserve who has trampled under foot the Son of God, and has regarded as unclean the blood of the covenant by which he was sanctified, and has insulted the Spirit of grace? . . . It is a terrifying thing to fall into the hands of the living God.* (Heb 10:28-31).

Our offense isn't just the things we have done or failed to do according to some moral code or law, it also includes any rejection of the Messiah. I doubt God will take lightly any situation where someone disregards the blood of Jesus, the Son of God, and says, whether verbally or through negligence, "Nah, it's not for me."

Our sins are against an eternal God, who extended to mankind an eternal covenant, and who also gave His eternal Son to suffer and die for us. Do we really believe that our rebellion deserves only a common slap on the wrist? In light of who God is and who He created us to be and who we have become in our sin, there is no end to our guilt and no end to how much we deserve death of every kind imaginable. It is for these many reasons that the Bible says that "the wages of sin is death" (Rom 6:23).

Christ is a Great Savior

This is a good time to bring up the Garden of Eden again. Do you remember that story, the original beauty and restfulness of man and woman's relationship in the presence of God? Do you recall the vastness of the fall that took place once they rebelled against Him and chose to disobey? Do you remember how God, although eventually needing to send them away, first graciously promised to send One who would be Victor over the serpent? Have you thought about the attempt of Adam and Eve to cover their guilt with their own efforts (the leaves) and God's subsequent, complete work on their behalf with the animal skins? Do you remember all of this?

Enter Jesus, the Son of God.

There are numerous books that effectively unpack the vast expanse and depth of what took place on the cross, where Jesus was executed.[1] As such, we will not go into that here. However, I will plainly restate these words of the Apostle Paul:

> *Now brothers, I want to clarify for you the Gospel I proclaimed to you. . . . For I passed on to you as most important what I also received: that Christ died for our sins according to the Scriptures, that He was buried, that He was raised on the third day according to the Scriptures. . .* (1 Cor 15:1-4, HCSB)

This is the Gospel that has been cherished by Christians for two millennia, as well as by those who, in veiled hope, came before it was realized in the chronology of human history. Aside from this one monumental thing, we will point out a couple of very important details about this atonement, this payment of Jesus for sins.

From the cross, just before He died, Jesus cried out "It is finished" (Jn 19:30). We must not forget that this was always the plan and the purpose for why Jesus came to live among us: "For this reason the Father loves me, because I lay down my life that I may take it up again." (Jn 10:17, ESV) The cry of completion from Jesus on the cross is a defining moment moment in God's dealings with our sin.

If Jesus was indeed suffering under our sin on the cross (Is 53), then His payment for sin was rendered complete as He cried out with these words. If we are indeed a human race of tremendous need in every way, especially in matters of sin, then this is the verse that says that God supplied for that need. If God wanted for us to have a Sabbath posture with regards to our own sin, then this is the verse that tells us how God has made a way. Jesus became the Sacrifice we needed. The work of forgiveness, although we were liable for our offenses, was fully and completed performed by Him.

The second detail worth mentioning from this portion of the book of John is how Jesus' work was completed just before a high Sabbath day. I have often read and heard about the significance of Jesus' atonement during the Passover feast, the importance of which, as I only briefly commented on earlier, simply cannot be overstated. However, at the same time, it is also noteworthy how a high Sabbath day followed soon after Jesus cried out in completion of His work and after He gave up His Spirit on the cross. It is enough to draw one's mind back to the Creation event, as it should.

It appears that God followed the same pattern both in the creation and in the redemption of those made in His image. Both were performed without our help and completely at the initiative of God. There was no lack in His redemptive work on the cross, just as there was no lack in his creative work at the very beginning. In the same way that God rested from His completed work after the Creation week (Gen 2:2-3), so He also rested from His completed work after atoning for sins (Heb 10:12-14).

As has been put forth all along, the Sabbath and the Gospel go together in ways that are so natural and life-giving that it is almost absurd that we've ever missed it. But, perhaps this is just another simple reminder that we are indeed utterly helpless people and that we so very easily forget. This is once again why God gave Sabbath to begin with—to serve as a regular and tangible reminder.

18

JESUS AND THE SABBATH: GOD AS LIFE

"It was the preparation day, and the Sabbath was about to begin. Now the women who had come with Him out of Galilee followed, and saw the tomb and how His body was laid. Then they returned and prepared spices and perfumes. And on the Sabbath they rested according to the commandment. But on the first day of the week, at early dawn, they came to the tomb bringing the spices which they had prepared. And they found the stone rolled away from the tomb, but when they entered, they did not find the body of the Lord Jesus." (Luke 23:54–24:3)

It seems clear by now that there are plentiful ways in which we need saving and easily double the number of reminders of our own inadequacy to do so. However, there's one example of this in particular that stands out at this point: death. If you think about it, in a way, all of our weaknesses eventually point us to the matter of death. It may sound like a stretch at first, but if you follow the thread long enough you'll get there. We examined sickness as probably the easiest and most tangible example and reminder of our mortality. But there are other ways that the sting of death pokes its head, even if indirectly.

Death Has Many Weapons

When you think about human suffering and misery, we are still ultimately talking about death. Allow me to explain. The Creation narrative presented to us in Genesis 1-2 is one of beauty, creativity, and life. It is exciting to read, and the soul begins to long for that type of existence, much like a subconscious reflex. We are creatures who crave life and purpose and vitality and creativity in every sense of the word. It is not enough to say that we crave only the absence of a physical death. Depression is a great example of this truth. Humans can wrestle with a prolonged sadness when faced with things like unemployment, indefinite daily monotony, limited human connection, purposelessness, human suffering, lack of personal fulfillment, boredom with uncreative forms of entertainment, and so on.

I truly believe that the image of God in us is why we love to take exciting risks, meet new people, explore cultures, dance, make music, paint new works, travel to outer space, savor new dishes, and sing at the top of our lungs in the car. . . with the windows up, of course. Although death is probably humanity's single greatest fear, there is more to it than the absence of physical life. That is, there is more to death than *just* physical death. Humans struggle with a type of death that is inward.

A simple proof of this is suicide—and, though I mention it only in passing, please do not misread me as speaking without the sobriety the topic deserves. Life can become so dull and so boring and so depressing and so, well, *lifeless* that some would rather end their life than continue on. Speaking as one with a dark personal history of depression and suicidal thoughts, I can confidently say that there are times when people actually view the loss of physical life as more valuable than keeping it in misery. Regardless of how we perceive and fear death, whether literally as the absence of physical life or figuratively as the nonexistence of abundant life (or joy), the completed works of Christ makes way for our Sabbath rest in Him.

History is replete with our attempts to ignore, avoid, delay, or overcome death. There are legends of waters that give eternal life. There have been "snake oil" salesmen who have hoodwinked the masses by telling them that their particular product is the cure for all that ails them. Modern medicine allows people to physically modify their bodies to give the illusion of youth, so that one might feel farther from death. We do death-*defying* stunts to remind ourselves that we will "exit stage left" on our own terms. In Western cultures, we have become increasingly (and perhaps absurdly) body and health conscious. Depending on which expert you ask, either everything or nothing is poisonous for use or consumption. We are either skeptical of modern medicine or, conversely, of the various oils, goo's, and potions meant to be more natural for our health. In one way or another, this points to the fact that we don't want to die, and we want our lives to be as abundant as possible.

But, here's the rub: we all still die. And we all still struggle to fight against a meaningless and lifeless existence. Despite our best efforts throughout history, we are still poor and needy, with nothing to offer when it comes to our unavoidable death. This is why the resurrection of Jesus is irreplaceable for Christians.

Jesus is Our Life

The Gospel of John provides a number of references to Jesus as the everlasting spring of resurrection life, starting from the very beginning: "Life was in Him, and that life was the light of men." (1:4, HCSB) Later on in the fifth chapter, the writer John gives an account of when Jesus healed a man on the Sabbath who had been ill for 38 years (5:1-15). The depiction of this man's situation—so debilitated that he is unable to get into the pool of healing on his own, but needs someone to put him in the water—is the perfect picture of the human condition. Without the life of Jesus, we are stranded on the island of death with no hope of rescue.

Of course, this healing by Jesus was a prime occasion for His opponents to persecute Him (5:16-18). One of His responses to them, "And just as the Father raises the dead and gives them life, so the Son also gives life to anyone He wants to." (5:21, HCSB) But Jesus is not clearly done with His lesson. He has more to say: He is the Agent of eternal life (5:24, 39-40) and He is the Giver of resurrection from death (5:25, 27-30). In fact, it has been granted by God, the Father, that He be the very quintessence of life itself (5:26). Later on in the Gospel of John, these declarations about Jesus' life-giving nature become even clearer when He raises a man named Lazarus from the dead (11:1-44). What was the lesson in all of this? "Jesus said to her [Martha], 'I am the resurrection and the life. The one who believes in Me, even if he dies, will live. Everyone who lives and believes in Me will never die—ever.'" (11:25-26, HCSB) And how did He prove it? He *Himself* died and rose again.

After Jesus atoned for our sins on a criminal's cross, He spent a high Sabbath day in a tomb, and then He bodily and victoriously rose from the grave on the third day. In one fell swoop, He forever overcame the sting of death by "laying death in His grave," as goes a lyric from one of my favorite songs.[1] This is one of the reasons why the Bible repeatedly speaks of resurrection in both a symbolic and spiritual sense, as well as in a literal and physical sense. That is, those united with Jesus in His death and resurrection experience an inward resurrection in the present and will also experience a physical resurrection to eternal life with Him.

Consider these words:

> *For we died and were buried with Christ by baptism. And just as Christ was raised from the dead by the glorious power of the Father, now we also may live new lives. Since we have been united with him in his death, we will also be raised to life as he was. We know that our old sinful selves were crucified with Christ so that sin might lose its power in our lives. We are no longer slaves to sin. For when we died with Christ we were set free from the power of sin. (Rom 6:4-7, NLT)*

These verses express that, because of the completed work of Jesus on our behalf, we no longer have reason to fear a physical death, nor do we have to fear a crippling and lifeless existence. Jesus overcame our physical death, which means that His claims for real life and for real relationship with God are trustworthy: "I came that they may have life, and have it abundantly" (Jn 10:10). He really is able "to save forever those who draw near to God through Him" (Heb 7:25).

This is the God who made all things new in the beginning through the act of creation, and who is also making all things new through redemption. The responsibility for all of this amazing creative and restorative work is on Him, not on us. Jesus is effectively bringing us back to the

Garden of Eden again, and He is doing so without our help, just as He intended it.

After all, He is not only the God of life, but He is also the God of the Sabbath and of the Gospel. He is the God who sustains the very beating of our hearts and every drawing of breath by our lungs, and He is also the One who gives life to our spiritual death (Rom 5:12-21) and who breathes the Holy Spirit into dry bones (Ezek 37:1-14). He is "the source of life" (Acts 3:15, HCSB) and He is the source of rest for those who trust in Him to work on their behalf.

19

JESUS AND THE SABBATH: GOD AS KING

*"Come, see the glorious works of the L*ORD*: See how he brings destruction upon the world. He causes wars to end throughout the earth. He breaks the bow and snaps the spear; he burns the shields with fire. 'Be still, and know that I am God! I will be honored by every nation. I will be honored throughout the world.'"* (Psalm 46:8-10, NLT)

During a period of 2017, when I initially wrote this chapter, America was experiencing a great deal of political turmoil, and it seemed that everyone had the solution.[1] This period of time was a tremendous shock to the country. In August, a White Nationalist rally was held of the campus on the University of Virginia, causing an uncontrollable firestorm of media attention, racial tension, and hate filled finger-pointing. Shortly after that, Hurricane Harvey swept the Gulf shores of Texas with devastating force, bringing unprecedented amounts of flooding, tragically claiming the lives of many, and causing untold amounts of damage. So, naturally, the two prominent sides of the political spectrum immediately began fighting about whether or not global warming was the cause.

Not long after, when various sports leagues began their seasons, some individuals and teams peacefully protested injustice by bucking some of the traditions surrounding the national anthem. Once again, people *en masse* began to turn on one another, with shouts and accusations taking many different forms, and the doomsday clock on the social media "witch trials" reset once again. As if all of that wasn't bad enough, late in the evening on Sunday, October 1, a man opened fire from the window of a Las Vegas hotel room into a crowd of thousands attending an open-air concert. All told, fifty-eight people died and another 489 were wounded.[2] It was an awful, awful thing to see on the news. How much worse must it have been to witness, or to be connected in some way to those victims? And, no sooner had it hit the TV, then the fighting started again. Whose fault was it? What legislation (or lack thereof) was to blame? When is all of this chaos going to end?

And all of that took place within a small window of about eight to ten weeks.

In many ways, it's understandable. We are creatures of emotion and, whether or not we still recognize the image of God in one another, we still act and react as though we do. Things like this shouldn't happen, and we need a reason. We need someone to blame. We need some kind of answer that is going to bring some sense into the equation. We need to feel secure again, to know that things will turn out alright in the end.

Our Inability to Save

If you're looking for words to explain that universally haunting question, "How can a good God let bad things happen?" this is the wrong book. We're not going to go down that road here, primarily because it is beyond the scope of this book. [Regardless, I don't know if anyone can supply an answer sufficient to satisfy the masses.] Nevertheless, it is easy to see, and we must come to grips with the fact that our world is filled with a certain amount of chaos. I've heard it put this way before: "You're either heading into a storm, or just coming out of one." It's a bit gloomy, sure, but it certainly feels true, doesn't it?

To add, we must not forget that an American is writing these words. I freely admit that, by and large, we experience better living conditions and higher levels of comfort than most in this world. The level of suffering that exists around the world today, outside of the cushy borders of the West, is simply shocking and gut-wrenching. And, yet, it's always been this way.

Did you ever notice that, once sin entered God's flawless world, it only took one generation for the first murder to take place? One. You can find the story in Genesis 4:1-16. It's tragic, and it was just the beginning of a world spiraling out of control. People have been dealing with these issues since our parents left the Garden of Eden. Are we really foolish enough to believe ourselves to be the first generation of people on the earth adequate enough to right the wrongs of this world? We shouldn't be. We have been trying to save ourselves from the beginning—trying to bring an end to the restlessness and homelessness we feel when we look around at our broken world.

Everyone has an opinion and everyone has a solution. How many times have you heard this statement, in one form or another: "If we could all just . . . then things would really start to change"? I've heard it more times that I can count. Our idealism, our best intentions, and our proposed solutions *never* produce the far-reaching results we had hoped for. Sometimes, we are so desperate for a solution to our problems and so blind to our own weaknesses, that we even forget the painful lessons of the past.

While we were living in Seattle, I used to see bills posted on light poles advocating for a number of causes and lifestyles. There was one in particular that caught my eye one day. Paraphrasing what I read, this flyer called for the end of oppression. It called-out the failed and broken systems that keep people from equal opportunity and from realizing their fullest potential. It called for a new system that would give people a level playing field to become who they were meant to be, without the control of abusive authority. It went on like this for several sentences. Do you want to know who was promoting this? It was a local Communist group! *Really?!* This representation of neo-Communists was calling for people to join because they were convinced that Marxist beliefs, ideals, and systems were the solution for ending systematic corruption, human suffering, and oppressive living. *Are you kidding me?!* When I pointed this out to my Russian neighbor at the time, he just shook his head in disbelief. Silly Americans. . .

I find it interesting that many of us cannot function properly or even be decent human beings to one another without this magical black liquid called "coffee." Yet, we have the audacity to think we can save this world, to think that we can bring about the heaven-on-earth that every single generation in history has imagined and called for, but ultimately failed to bring about. We are convinced that *we* are the solution to the chronic problems we face—racism, pedophilia, starvation, genocide, sexism, ageism, rape, predatory lending, xenophobia, murder, abortion, war, poverty, human trafficking, and so on—while forgetting that we are the very cause of these things to begin with.

If we were meant to be stewards on this earth,[3] then we have seriously failed in our responsibilities, especially in caring for those who are made in God's image. We have collectively torn one another to pieces, slandering and murdering each other with our hatred and our prejudices, while foolishly calling out to God in the way of Cain: "Am I my brother's keeper?" (Gen 4:9, ESV).

Please do not misunderstand me. There is a real reason to celebrate those very fine moments in human history when God's grace led people and nations down a path that honored the image of God in others.[4] Nevertheless, those amazing victories still fell short of the worldwide impact we all long for. Those inspiring moments failed to bring about a universal freedom. It is a tough pill to swallow, but we must accept that we are deluded about the greatness of our own abilities and strengths, both individually and collectively. Simply put, we must accept that we cannot save the world. But who can?

God's Ability to Save

Throughout the Bible, we see the answer: God will one day make the world right. Not only is He the only one who is powerful enough, He is also the only one righteous enough to execute justice properly on the earth. Psalm 46 is one of many parts of the Bible that communicates this truth. God is said to be a refuge or hiding place for His people in the midst of a world in turmoil (46:1, 4-5, 7). This goes for times of natural disaster (46:2-3), as well as for times when the turbulence of the world is caused by people and nations (46:6). He is also the God who will end all wars and make the restlessness of the nations to cease (46:8-9).

In another part of the Old Testament, the God of

Israel is portrayed at the One who will take the weapons of war that we have created[5] and transform them into plow-shares and pruning hooks (Is 2:2-4). It is a very powerful image if you think about it. The world we were originally created for was a beautiful one, where our primary work was to tend to the land. But, in our rebellion, we were forced out of the Garden of Eden and our conflicts began. Throughout history, weapons have been a powerful image of man's propensity to violence and war. And God is the one who will take these implements of death and turn them into tools used for gardening. Don't miss the fact that God is ultimately saying that He will take humanity back to the Garden. But how will God do this?

The answer is Jesus.

No King but Jesus

Jesus is the one who brings peace to the source of our conflict. This is why He is called the "Prince of Peace" in the Bible (Is 9:6). We are at war with God and at war with one another. Jesus ends our war with God though His death, burial, and resurrection for sins. Through this completed work, we can be forgiven and restored to God, no longer under his wrath and judgment. We can be taken back into the relationship that was broken in the Garden. Jesus, the Christ, is also able to end the wars we wage against one another. He is able to bring peace between individuals, within families, and among tribes of people. History has many examples of how faith in Christ has been the direct cause of healing and restoration of marriages, estranged families, neighboring clans with a history of feuding, and so on.

What really sets Jesus apart, however, is the scale on which He will bring about peace. After all, we must be consistent. If we are to say such great historical works of men and women fell short because they lacked a universal scope, then it had better be demonstrated that Jesus is different in this way as well. This is one of the reasons why the Bible, especially the book of the Revelation, goes through painstaking detail to outline and describe Jesus as the King who will not only end all wars and rule all nations, but He will do so forever. The images, although mysterious at times, are rather powerful in communicating the extent of Jesus' peaceful reign and what it takes to get there.

> *And I saw heaven opened, and behold, a white horse, and He who sat on it is called Faithful and True, and in righteousness He judges and wages war. His eyes are a flame of fire, and on His head are many diadems; and He has a name written on Him which no one knows except Himself. He is clothed with a robe dipped in blood, and His name is called The Word of God. And the armies which are in heaven, clothed in fine linen, white and clean, were following Him on white horses. From His mouth comes a sharp sword, so that with it He may strike down the nations, and He will rule them with a rod of iron; and He treads the wine press of the fierce wrath of God, the Almighty. And on His robe and on His thigh He has a name written, "KING OF KINGS, AND LORD OF LORDS."* (Rev 19:11-16)

This work of making all wars to end belongs to God. If that is truly the case, then what is our part? What is our work? Do we just sit around and do nothing all the time? Do we become inactive players in human history? To answer, we look back to the Scripture at the beginning of the chapter: "Be still, and know that I am God!" (Ps 46:10, NLT). Our primary job is to cease, stop, and desist in our striving, our turmoil, and our restlessness.

The rationale is that God says on two occasions in Psalm 46, "I will," to indicate that *He* is the One who will bring the peace that we crave, that the world craves. He is the One who will bring about the world that was meant to be. Therefore, we need to humbly recognize that our efforts are useless unless we are first at rest in Him. Again, this is not to downplay history's gains or contributions to human flourishing. It is to put them in their proper perspective. We can rest (46:10a) because God promises to be the Savior of this world and of history: "I will be honored by every nation. I will be honored throughout the world. (46:10b, NLT) We would be wise to be at rest and let Him to do His work.

Evoking this promise does not mean in any way, shape, or form that we are to cease our work entirely in this world. The Bible is also clear that people have an active and meaningful role on this earth and in this life. It is indeed a sad state, and dishonoring to God even, when the lives of supposed Christians reflect the biting, albeit potentially misinformed, lyrics: "you're so heavenly minded, you're no earthly good."[6] The power that Jesus carried with Him, the power that brought the future realities of the kingdom of God into real time, is the same power that is within Christians through the Holy Spirit. We are specifically gifted and charged to show to the world here and now, albeit only a shadow, what the future kingdom will be like for all eternity.

Nevertheless we have to remember that, whatever our work may be, it can and should come forth *only* from a heart that is at rest in God's promises that He will complete the work. If we refuse to believe this, we will be either prone to despair when our efforts to make a better world don't have the effect that we hoped, or prone to pride when things appear to go exactly the way we had hoped and planned. If we choose to work and toil as though the world depends on us, we will vacillate between the two, depending on how well we're doing that day. God has promised to complete this work of bringing peace to the world, between peoples and nations. This is meant to give us a sense of stillness. It is yet another promise that we can rest in while practicing Sabbath.

20

THE NEW CREATION AND THE SABBATH

"Then I saw a new heaven and a new earth . . . And I saw the holy city, new Jerusalem, coming down out of heaven from God . . . And I heard a loud voice from the throne, saying, 'Behold, the tabernacle of God is among men, and He will dwell among them, and they shall be His people, and God Himself will be among them, and He will wipe away every tear from their eyes; and there will no longer be any death; there will no longer be any mourning, or crying, or pain; the first things have passed away.' And He who sits on the throne said, 'Behold, I am making all things new.' . . . Then He said to me, 'It is done. I am the Alpha and the Omega, the beginning and the end. I will give to the one who thirsts from the spring of the water of life without cost.'"
(Revelation 21:1-6)

For many of us, it can be hard to imagine the world we know returning to paradise, to a state of overall and unblemished goodness. The prior chapter sought to convey that God has promised and will indeed bring about restoration to the world, primarily in ending wars and bringing peace. He will heal our relationships and our dealings with one another. This chapter is related, but differs slightly in that it primarily focuses on the earth and on the Creation *itself*.

To borrow some crude designations that I've come across, I do not consider myself a "tree hugger" or a person who thinks animals are people, too. Having said this, I am grateful that God has significantly changed my mind regarding how I perceive the created order that He has gifted to a world of image-bearers. When we recall Genesis 1, Adam and Eve were given the charge to *both* enjoy *and* be stewards of the earth and all it contains (1:26-31). Seeing that this is a direct command from God, I think it wise to listen. But, looking at the world around us, it seems pretty obvious that we have done a pretty lousy job of taking care of God's planet. Again, I'm not talking about people here; I'm talking about the earth itself.[1]

Dropping the Ball of Stewardship

Did you know that there is a floating island of trash in the Pacific Ocean, at least one-and-a-half times the size of Texas? Did you know that, although the sizes vary, there are five of these floating tropical islands occupying our oceans?[2] Did you know that there is a landfill in India that can easily be mistaken for a mountain "because it holds 10 million tons of garbage now piled higher than the city's skyline"?[3] Only thirty years or so ago, there was a terrifying hole in the world's ozone layer; thankfully, it has since been drastically reduced.[4] Sections of rainforests about half the size of England vanish each year due to reckless deforestation, leading some to believe that the current rate might leave our planet without our rainforests in about 100 years.[5] And this is to say nothing about the many other environmental issues related to: wasteful consumerism, illegal dumping, oil industry regulation, strip mining, fracking, the effects of pollution on the Great Barrier Reef, and more.

Let us put politics aside for a moment and simply acknowledge that this sure does not sound like what God had in mind when He created the world, made man and woman in His image, and then charged them to steward the earth (implicitly) as He would. We have done quite a harmful number on this planet, and we really don't have any excuse for it. We are especially culpable if we choose to look at all that we have done and grow deaf and blind to our effect on our surroundings, and to the consequences of failing to have a change of heart about these things.

Take this scenario, and now imagine it being wholly the responsibility of humanity to restore the earth back to its original state, or else we're all in for it. The thought is depressing, as it is frankly an impossible feat. But, isn't that what it means to be a steward? One person is responsible for taking care of what actually belongs to another. In this case, however, we're talking about being stewards of God's Creation.

I have heard and read conservationist and ecological representatives tell of irreparable damage having already been done to the environment, and the only thing we can do is to move forward with what remains. Of course, it is hard to know about these things with absolute certainty. Yet, isn't the fact that we're even having this conversation indictment enough? We have really shown our true colors —our ineptitude, inability, and indifference to caring for what God has entrusted to us.

Is all hope lost? Well, yes and no.

. . .

Making All Things New

Like all the other issues we have discussed (e.g. health, human relationships, etc.) there is an inherent lostness to the situation because sin has entered the world. Even though we can engage in great works to help care for the environment, it will *never* be restored to its original state and intention. That ship sailed a long time ago. This is the hopeless part. However, even though the Bible indicates this sad reality, it also speaks of God's promise to make a new earth (Isa 65:17; 66:22; 2 Pet 3:13; Rev 21:1). This is the good news, the part where hope is *not* lost.

The God of the Bible is an expert at performing the works that we are unable to do. This includes the works that were actually charged to us to begin with, like caring for the earth. Part of our sin against God is the reckless negligence we have shown with regards to His creation, but even that will be redeemed by Him through Jesus Christ. All of our gross unfaithfulness in every area of life has been swallowed up forever by His completed works. We can be at rest in this truth.

As such, if you are troubled by what you see happening to the physical creation, then God has given you the gift of Sabbath. This gift was given to regularly remind you of and encourage you in the Gospel, the good news that He can not only make *you* new—right now, even, should you call on Him (Rom 10:13)—but also that He has promised to one day make *all things* new, including this physical world. Although the fulfillment of a new earth has clearly not taken place yet, this future hope can and should be considered good-as-done because God has promised it; and He never lies.

Reversing the Curse

It is amazing how the first three chapters of the Bible are harmoniously similar to the final three chapters of the Bible, except in a kind of reverse order. The first three chapters of Genesis tell how: God creates the world (1:1–2:3); people enjoy unhindered fellowship with Him (2:4-25); the serpent deceives the man and woman (3:1-6); sin's curse enters the world (3:7-19); the earth begins to fall apart (3:17-18); death enters the world (3:19); and the man and woman are sent away from the presence of God (3:22-24).

The final three chapters of Revelation describe the process of God taking all that has become bad, and then undoing it. God's enemy is bound and sent away forever (20:1-10); and the evil of the world, including people,[6] is sent away forever (20:11-15). God brings about a new heaven, a new earth, and a new Jerusalem, all of which are joined together (21:1-2, 9-27). Death is abolished (21:4); sin's curse is abolished (22:3); and God's people are forever in His presence again (21:3-4; 22:3-4). To summarize, this creating and redeeming God comprehensively makes *all things new* (21:5). And, at this end of this, He says the words, "It is done" (21:6). Sound familiar?

God insists on making all things new because that is how they should be, and also because we are not able to do so. We have seen over and over again that He is gladly able to do what we are not. It has always been this way. This is the God of the Sabbath and of the Gospel. He completes His works and rests, so that we might first enjoy His rest and, from *out of that rest*, engage in the work given to us.

In light of this, therefore, our practice of Sabbath is also intended to be a regular reminder that this God makes all things new. He has promised, and so He will do it . . . without fail.

21

THE SABBATH AND THE GOSPEL, PART 2

"So there remains a Sabbath rest for the people of God. For the one who has entered His rest has himself also rested from his works, as God did from His. Therefore let us be diligent to enter that rest . . ." (Hebrews 4:9-11a)

All throughout the ages, the LORD God has been calling His people to Sabbath. This invitation began with Adam and Eve and their descendants. Later, it was extended to the family and nation of Israel, whom God chose and spoke to long ago. Even in their rebellion, God continued to offer them rest. This invitation was passed on to the early Church, those first among God's people to receive the gift of the permanently indwelling Holy Spirit. And, today, the invitation has been extended to us. Those of us who are in union with Christ have entered into God's rest. Hebrews 4:9-11 states this for readers just in case it wasn't already clear enough.[1] But why has God made it so?

I hope by now the answer is clear. The doctrinal magnitude of the Sabbath is so immense that it cannot be exaggerated. This is because it is intimately intertwined with the Gospel, and the importance of the Gospel cannot be overstated. The two go hand-in-hand in many ways, which is why we began this journey with the statement: *The Sabbath is a gracious gift from God. Its primary purpose is to point the world to the Gospel—to both prepare the heart for it and to cultivate life in it. The Sabbath does so by reminding us that:*

1. there is a work of some kind that desperately needs to be done;
2. we are utterly helpless to perform it;
3. God is not only perfectly able to complete it, but He has already done so or promised to do so;
4. as a result of His promised or completed works, God's people are to assume a posture of rest in every facet and season of life; and
5. if there is any subsequent work to which God has called His people, it is to be performed only from that posture of rest.

Such weighty truths will naturally have positive, practical outworking, which is why we concluded by saying: *The regular practice of Sabbath reminds us of our great need for the rest that only God can give; it encourages others among the people of God; and it gives credible testimony to a restless world in dire need of the Gospel.*

Jesus Is All-in-All

God Himself is the great Creator, Worker, Servant, Healer, Light, Savior, Sacrifice, Life, and King that our world—including all its lowly (though still image-bearing) inhabitants—desperately needs. The Gospel, the "good news" from God, speaks specifically to the death, burial, and resurrection of Jesus for our sins (1 Cor 15:1-4), as well as to the many implications of such news. This completed work of Jesus is the most explicit and essential understanding of Gospel at which we can arrive.

Still, the Gospel pattern was established long before Jesus was incarnated into the world. This pattern highlights our tremendous need and, in the face of that need, God's far-surpassing greatness and provision. Over and over again, our overarching weakness and incapability is shown to necessitate a work of the God who saves. Thankfully, this saving God is pleased to work on our behalf because He loves us. He wants us to rest in His care and in the truth that all of His works are either complete or effectively-so because He has promised a future completion. Accordingly, the letter to the Hebrews states:

> So there is a special rest still waiting for the people of God. For all who have entered into God's rest have rested from their labors, just as God did after creating the world. So let us do our best to enter that rest. (4:9-11, NLT)

God's works are complete, so He Himself is our rest. And so, our aim is to enter that rest.

The purpose and core message of Sabbath is outlined throughout the Bible. The Sabbath pattern given to us by God points to, prepares for, and cultivates life in the Gospel. Our need for Sabbath has never ceased, nor has God's desire for us to remember and to practice it. He does not want us to do so *in order that* we can serve Him, but *as a result of* the fact that He already served us first. "Love consists in this: not that we loved God, but that He loved us and sent His Son to be the propitiation for our sins." (1 Jn 4:10, HCSB) To ignore the Sabbath or to carry about in the exercise of it with any other perspective would profane it, to rob it of its very essence and meaning.

By now, I hope and pray that you have become convinced of what God has convinced me of. If you have, I am grateful, but not because I won some kind of argument. Rather, it is because I believe that you and I are that much closer to a joyful practice of resting in the completed works of Jesus. And, if you have become convinced, then you may also be wondering what this looks like in real time. What might Sabbath look like in the everyday rhythms of life?

It is on these practical matters that we begin to draw to a close.

22

PRACTICING SABBATH: A MATTER OF FAITH

"For only we who believe can enter his rest. As for the others, God said, 'In my anger I took an oath: "They will never enter my place of rest,"' even though this rest has been ready since he made the world. We know it is ready because of the place in the Scriptures where it mentions the seventh day: 'On the seventh day God rested from all his work.' . . ."
(Hebrews 4:3-5, NLT)

This chapter as well as the next deal with the practical side of Sabbath. The goal is to begin answering the question, "What does it actually look like to do this thing?" The first chapter is dedicated entirely to the matter of faith, for reasons that should soon become clear. The second chapter attempts to explore this in life's various rhythms: daily, weekly, monthly, annually, and seasonally. By God's grace, when we are finished, our Sabbath practice should be more attainable, purposeful, and energizing than we have ever experienced before. So, let's get to it.

. . .

Repent and Believe the Gospel

Faith is a paramount theme all the way through the Bible. It is written in the Hebrews letter that "without faith it is impossible to please Him [God]" (11:6). It was always fundamental. For this reason, a number of New Testament writers tell of the faith of Abraham (Rom 4:3; Gal 3:6; Jas 2:23), a predecessor to the nation of Israel. In these New Testament recollections, Abraham was said to be given a righteous standing before God because he believed Him (Gen 15:6) even though, humanly speaking, his time was well before Jesus. This is why the Lord repeatedly called people to a real and saving faith (Lk 5:20; 7:50), as well as why His followers did the same (Rom 1:17; 3:22; Heb 10:38). Take, for example, this call to faith in the letter to the Ephesians:

> *God saved you by his grace when you believed. And you can't take credit for this; it is a gift from God. Salvation is not a reward for the good things we have done, so none of us can boast about it.* (2:8-9, NLT)

Whether speaking of persons in the days of the Old and New Testaments, or of someone in the 21st century, the Bible is clear that the only means by which someone is right with their Creator is by way of faith.

Conversely, the Bible is also clear that, for those who do not believe, there is only a horrifying expectation for the future. If the positive expression of faith is that those who practice it will enter into God's rest, then the opposite is also true. Those who do not exercise faith will *not* enter into God's rest. The end of the Bible tells us that God will make a final judgment on all peoples. Those who were unbelieving and those whose worship was not directed towards their Creator, have a terrible fate in Hell:

"And the smoke of their torment goes up forever and ever, and they have no rest, day or night" (Rev 14:11, ESV).

Faith is essentially taking God at His word because you trust Him—His integrity, His ability, and His faithfulness—to do what He promises to do. Or, put into other words: "faith is the assurance of things hoped for, the conviction of things not seen" (Heb 11:1). Saving faith that is described in the Bible is not some ambiguous, throwaway version, but a real and even visceral one. We belabor this point because it is essential in the conversation about Sabbath. We must understand that *the primary work and labor of the Christian is faith*.

As inherently self-righteous people, we are edgy and eager to do something to contribute to the betterment of ourselves and this world because, at least in part, we can ultimately wear it like a badge of honor. Our motives are never totally pure, and we enjoy and seek out the praise of other people. Along these lines, we can also fall into the dangerous trap of believing that God will somehow be impressed with our deeds, completely forgetting the warning of the prophets: "We are all infected and impure with sin. When we display our righteous deeds, they are nothing but filthy rags." (Is 64:6, NLT)

The Primary Work of (Childlike) Faith

If you want to follow the saving God of the Bible, the first thing you must do is repent and shut down this striving after works and trust Him by faith. You and I, we must believe what God has said to us. This means we must exercise faith in God's work through His Son, Jesus Christ. We must believe that He not only did it on our behalf, but also that the work is so complete that we have nothing to offer in order to improve it. Consider this word from our ancestors in the faith:

> *He is able, once and forever, to save those who come to God through him . . . Unlike those other high priests, he does not need to offer sacrifices every day. They did this for their own sins first and then for the sins of the people. But Jesus did this once for all when he offered himself as the sacrifice for the people's sins.* (Heb 7:25-27, NLT)

The work is complete. It was taken care of for us because we were unable. And we simply have to accept it because that is what faith does. And that faith is what pleases God.

It is not at all different from the relationship between a child and a parent. Children are entirely dependent upon their parents for survival. And, ideally, we parents do not begrudge our children for this but, rather, find it an unending joy to care for their needs and see that they grow and thrive. This type of parental relationship is why Jesus openly confronted anyone, including His very own disciples, who tried to keep little ones away from Him. The explanation for this: "Let the children come to me. Don't stop them! For the kingdom of Heaven belongs to those who are like these children." (Mt 19:14, NLT) Children provide the ideal picture of dependence, which is to be emulated by all of humanity towards the Heavenly Father. Otherwise, only a sharp rebuke remains.

The historically eminent Jonathan Edwards, studied by both Christians and non- for his immense influence on (pre-) American culture and on Western culture in general, once received a letter from an eighteen year old, named Dorothy Hatheway. His insightful response to her was eventually published and, among the numerous points (nineteen!) he provided in order to counsel this young lady, one of the most personally profound for me was with regards to faith. He urged her to remain vigilant in the faith and make war on pride—that which is "the worst viper that is in the heart, the greatest disturber of the soul's peace and sweet communion with Christ . . . the most difficulty rooted out, and is the most hidden, secret and deceitful of all lusts"—with the indispensible weapon of humility before God.[1]

One of the world's foremost Edwards historians and biographers, George M. Marsden, quoted and commented on this particular letter:

> *Ultimately . . . one had to become as a child taking the wounded hand of the gentle Christ: "In all your course, walk with God and follow Christ as a little, poor, helpless child, taking hold of Christ's hand, keeping your eye on the mark of the wounds on his hands and side, whence came the blood that cleanses you from sin and hiding your nakedness under the skirt of the white shining robe of his righteousness."*[2]

It is profound to think that this teenager who, in contrast to our culture's ever-expanding designation of "adolescence," in those days would have already been considered an adult—though will have not been too far removed from childhood—was instructed to be ever-child-like in her faith and trust towards Jesus, the Son of God. As she grew further into adulthood, the greatest threat was pride, that is, a growing sense of independence from God. And, that which could save her from such a destructive state of self-sufficiency was an ongoing and growing commitment to childlike dependence on and faith in her Lord and Savior.

. . .

The Hard Work of Faith

I anticipate that we will inwardly fight this because it goes against what we have been taught. Some of us grew up with empty religious platitudes like, "God helps those who help themselves," which have only fed the self-righteous tendencies within us. But those empty words must be rejected and repented of, and we must choose to come to a full stop. I assure you, making the choice to cease customary attitudes and works *for* God—and, in turn, making faith your primary work—is a lot harder than you would think. This is why we are told, "let us *be diligent* to enter that rest" (Heb 4:11, emphasis mine). Faith is to be our primary focus, and faith is hard work. It will take nearly all of our energy just to believe what God says is true. And, due to our overwhelming weakness, that work will almost constantly feel attacked and may even appear at times to ominously teeter on the precipice of ruin.

Elisabeth Elliot was a highly influential figure in recent Christian history, all the way up to and now after her death in 2015. Some of her personal hardships, such as the martyrdom of her first husband, Jim, have even had a significant impact on culture at large, including those who would not claim the Christian faith. Her writings are widely read and cherished but, even in saying this, it is important to remember that much of the gain that others have experienced from her life came at a tremendous cost to her and others around her.

One of her influential works is *These Strange Ashes*, wherein Elliot recounts some key lessons from her first year as a missionary in San Miguel de los Colorados. Those lessons, she writes, revolve around the matter of faith and the question of whether or not she could and would trust in God's sovereignty. That is, when afflicted by the varying degrees of suffering that life can bring, especially if one

chooses to follow Jesus of Nazareth, the rejected and crucified One, will faith stand the test? Will faith prove true and
endure?

One of those many hard lessons in trusting God left
her with the observation:

> *Faith's most severe tests come not when we see nothing, but when*
> *we see a stunning array of evidence that seems to prove our faith*
> *vain. If God were God, if He were omnipotent, if He had cared,*
> *would this have happened? . . . One turns in disbelief again from*
> *the circumstances and looks into the abyss. But in the abyss there is*
> *only blackness, no glimmer of light, no answering echo.*[3]

Those are dark and ominous thoughts. When one
reads her account, along with the stories of other well-
known historical Christian figures that have likewise
suffered and subsequently wrestled with doubts and fears,
it is impossible to conclude that biblical faith is a "walk in
the park." Rather, faith in the God of the Bible is hard,
hard work. In fact, it pushes us to our limits and then
shoves us over the edge of the cliff and into the unknown.
It is a lifelong grind that can often feel more like death
than victory but, thankfully and even paradoxically, God
says is the only way to experience true, abundant, and
eternal life.

Make no mistake: faith will be the most strenuous exercise during our days on this earth.

The Security of Faith

Considering these things, perhaps it is more precise to
say that faith will not just take nearly all of our energy but,
rather, faith will take *more than* all of our energy. It should
be no surprise then that we are told in the Bible that faith

itself, in its entirety, is a gift from and a work of God. Both our personal and our communal faith finds its beginning, as well as its completion, in Him alone:

> *Let us also lay aside every weight, and sin which clings so closely, and let us run with endurance the race that is set before us, looking to Jesus, the founder and perfecter of our faith, who for the joy that was set before him endured the cross, despising the shame, and is seated at the right hand of the throne of God.* (Heb 12:1-2, ESV)

Did you notice the mysterious mix within those two verses?

On one hand, there is the gritty battle of faith in which we must be personally engaged and unrelenting. On the other hand, we clearly see the portrayal of Jesus as both the Author and Perfector of the faith that is within us. This incredible truth is one of the reasons why those of us in Christ do not have to worry or fret about the perseverance of our faith. This is the case even though we are indeed simultaneously, but not contradictorily, commanded to "continue to work out your salvation with fear and trembling" (Php 2:12, ESV). The reason is because, from the following verse, even though we labor in faith, we do so knowing that "it is God who works in you, both to will and to work for his good pleasure" (Php 2:13, ESV). Just as He has in every other area of our lives, Jesus has taken full ownership of making sure that our faith not only begins in earnest, but that it also makes it through the finish line. Believing these things takes faith; and this faith must be essential to us. In fact, it must be held as most precious.

Considering this, we must also sensitive to the fact that people have the uncanny desire and tendency to take just about anything and treat it like a commodity—to aggregate and then leverage in exchange for goods and services from God. Sadly, but unsurprisingly, this can happen with faith as well. Many people have wounded others and/or have been deeply wounded by these types of practices,[4] myself included on both counts. Constantly worrying about our respective measure of faith, including what it is or is not producing, can be crippling and is by no means what God had in mind. Biblical faith does not do this because the faith described in the Scriptures is both resting and learning to be at rest in the completed works of Christ.

Real faith learns to trust God for how one is created, warts and all. Real faith learns to trust God regarding the circumstances of upbringing, regardless of how painful. Real faith learns to how to trust God with global turmoil, embarrassing or oppressive national leaders, and current events. Real faith learns how to believe God's goodness in all circumstances, and even to praise Him in them. Real faith trusts God even with the matter of salvation, that He is truly able to save you and me forever and ever. Real faith trusts God with the process of sanctification, that we are presently tarnished *imago Dei* works of art that God is restoring: "For I am confident of this very thing, that He who began a good work in you will perfect it until the day of Christ Jesus" (Php 1:6). Real faith learns to trust that Jesus is indeed the Good Shepherd (Jn 10:11), always present and always leading, whether in a disturbingly dark valley or surrounded by refreshing green grass and quiet waters (Ps 23). The list goes on and on.

If you and I read that list with any sincerity and integrity, we will quickly realize how hard of a work faith really is. It is the primary work that God has given to His people: to believe, to trust. And we will need every ounce of spiritual energy (and more) to do this because faith is a battle. Our weakness will be ever-present and we will continue to easily forget; so, it is okay (and normal) when we need to cry out like the father of the demon possessed boy: "I do believe; help my unbelief" (Mk 9:24). And while we labor in faith, we must remember that God has worked and is working on our behalf to bring about a completion that can only be brought about by Him.

For this reason, not to mention the many others, the regular practice of Sabbath is vital to our life in Christ. The choice to regularly and appropriately "cease and desist" reminds us of the rest that Jesus has already given us, even as it relates to the security of our salvation in Him. This gift from God is meant to be a rhythmic and enduring reminder for us to assume a Gospel-centered posture in every area of life. To be clear, the type of faith described in the Bible is meant to (super-) naturally produce other works (Jas 2:17). However, *beginning with* and *working from* faith is indispensable and non-negotiable.

23

PRACTICING SABBATH: TAKING ACTION

"The faith which you have, have as your own conviction before God. Happy is he who does not condemn himself in what he approves. But he who doubts is condemned if he eats, because his eating is not from faith; and whatever is not from faith is sin." (Romans 14:22-23)

This chapter is *not* about common spiritual exercises like sharing the Gospel (evangelism), mercy ministry, social justice causes, teaching, preaching, or any other good work that can be engaged in for our saving God. That is beyond the scope of this book, and there are already numerous resources available that speak adequately on those topics. We will speak more broadly and on other matters.

We will begin with the assumption that these works are borne out of a restful faith, which is the theological foundation that we sought to lay in the preceding chapters of this book. We want to make sure that every activity is performed out of an attitude of Sabbath rest in Christ. Even where I do attempt to speak practically, please remember that I am not doing so comprehensively. I'm only scratching the surface of the vast number of ways that this can play out in the everyday rhythms of life. Nevertheless, the underlying principles that follow should help lead one to some helpful application that extends well beyond the limited examples provided.

To further explain, I will give a quick example. The Prologue of this book detailed a bit of our family's journey to start a new church in Seattle, including my mindset in the midst of it. When we moved from Kansas to Washington State in January 2014, we had a choice to make. When we labored for Jesus, what would our motivation be? What would our posture be? Would we work with a restless anxiety that believes everything is dependent on us? Would we believe that God is somehow more pleased with us because of our efforts? Or, conversely, would we first believe the words of Christ, that He will indeed "build His church" (Mt 16:18) and will be with us (Mt 28:18-20)? Would we *first* find our rest in Him and *then* proceed into our work? There is a vast difference between the two. Motivation is everything. Motivation affects how we care for people and for the Creation, and it especially affects how we glorify God in our works for Him.

Additional Resources

Lastly, before we proceed, I would like to make mention of an additional resource that I found helpful in some of my later research for this book: *Sabbath Keeping*, written by Lynne M. Baab. While this final chapter provides some helpful examples for practicing Sabbath, Baab's book on the whole focuses more on providing useful tips for application. She not only draws on the lessons learned from her own decades-long practice of Sabbath, she also includes the contributions and input of dozens of others who have done the same. Her bibliography and her "For Further Reading" appendix reveal that she's done her homework. I'm not naturally very creative, and can easily settle into routines that run the risk of becoming stale. Therefore, her book was very helpful in challenging me to further expand the "how" of practicing Sabbath. As I said in the beginning, I'm not interested in reinventing the wheel. I have attempted to lay a lot of theological groundwork here, seasoned with a dash of varied practical considerations, and now I happily recommend her book as a great follow-up if you've never read it.

On Daily Sabbath

When the Hebrews letter speaks of a Sabbath rest that still "remains for the people of God," I believe that it points primarily (but not only) to an attitude of the heart. Every day, the follower of Jesus needs a heart that is oriented to the Gospel. I am a firm believer that Christians should preach the Gospel to themselves daily or, perhaps more accurately, several times a day. Remember, we are weak and prone to forgetfulness, even in those matters which are most foundational.

Therefore, whatever form our spiritual disciplines take —Bible reading or listening, quiet meditation, confession and repentance, prayer (both speaking and listening), fasting, and more—they need to happen *as a result of* rest in the Gospel. Naturally, this Gospel mentality extends beyond personal devotional exercises. Whatever you are doing— running or lifting weights, sharing a meal with friends, writing a TPS report for work,[1] studying for a test, spending time with neighbors, playing with your kids, writing a song for your dog, getting a beer with your co-

workers, or even enjoying some time in front of the TV—
the idea is that you do it in faith. Whatever one does, it is
to be from a posture and mindset of rest in the already
completed works of God on our behalf.

It is as though we are actively reminding ourselves (and
perhaps even praying): "I think I am going to do [activity
A, B, and C] today, but *not* because I think God will love
me more if I succeed. And, furthermore, I think I am
going to try and keep away from [activity X, Y, and Z], but
not because I think He will love me less if I fail; I just don't
think it would be wise or honoring to His name. So, I will
do some things (and refrain from others) because I believe
that He has already fully and completely loved and
accepted me through His Son, Jesus." Though these
thoughts and prayers are admittedly a little ungainly in the
form I've written them, they reaffirm that can we only truly
fulfill the purposes of Christ from a restful heart. Or, as the
Apostle Paul explained it: "whatever is not from faith is
sin" (Rom 14:23); and "whether you eat or drink, or whatever you do, do it all for the glory of God" (1 Cor
10:31, NLT).

Do not be surprised if you have to pray in that way
several times a day. After all, faith is hard, and it is especially challenging for innately self-righteous people like us.
Nevertheless, it must be done. We must make daily
Sabbath rest a reality in our lives. If you consider yourself
especially new to this line of thinking, let me encourage
you to ponder very little on what you can do for God, especially early on. Instead, spend as much time as possible
thinking about what He has done for you. If you do this, I
believe that the other stuff will follow more naturally.

Aside from this, make it a priority to build patterns into
your day that help demonstrate this rest, this faith and trust
in God's complete and satisfying provision. Prioritize a

posture of rest early on in the day, from which you can launch into that which God has given you to do. Make the effort to establish appropriate boundaries in your work day and in your relationships so that these critical areas of life can reflect trust in the completed works of Christ.

On Weekly Sabbath

This is a big one. We may do well at daily Sabbath, but we will eventually tire out. We are just weak people. Our minds and bodies weren't meant to go on-and-on without rest. God knew this and, therefore, provided us with an opportunity for weekly Sabbath. We wear out in all kinds of ways. Therefore, I wholeheartedly believe that restoration takes places on multiple levels—spiritual, mental, emotional, physical, relational, and more—when we practice Sabbath.

Practicing weekly Sabbath is not essential for receiving God's love and favor. That matter was already *fully accomplished* for us through the work of Christ, including through the perfect fulfillment of God's Law. However, I do believe that making Sabbath a weekly priority (as much as possible) is an act of faith-driven obedience to God. After all, faith and works go together, like two sides of the same coin (Jas 2:17, 26). There is a type of pleasure that God has when our faith turns into practical expression.[2] As the Apostle John writes: "If anyone says, 'I love God,' and hates his brother, he is a liar; for he who does not love his brother whom he has seen cannot love God whom he has not seen." (1 Jn 4:20, ESV)

Accordingly, I believe that every Christian everywhere should do everything they can to create space for practicing Sabbath one day a week, whether it be all on one calendar day or split up between two days. I believe that

Christians, churches, small groups, families, and whoever else, should make this a priority. Again, you will not be loved by God any more by doing so, just as you will not be loved any less by not doing so. However, you will be obeying God in faith, which brings a kind of pleasure to God. Not to mention, you will be much healthier in just about every area of life.

This means doing what it takes to make sure it happens for you, as well as for others. Some will have to learn how to say a holy "no" to some opportunities, even really good ones. Husbands will have to watch the kids for several hours to make sure their wives get some extended alone-time with Jesus. Small groups or family members will need to rally around single moms (or dads) to assist with child-care and even finances, if necessary, to help make sure that these superheroes get the weekly break that they need. This could mean turning down extra hours at work, or inconveniently shifting the work week around. This means that procrastination needs to be less-and-less present in the lives of college students, so that they can carve out a full day to rest. Some sports fans may need to give up a game every now and again. Some people will need to take a break from giving work projects to their spouses—the bathroom remodel can wait. Families may need to make extra efforts to coordinate their calendars and busy schedules. If you are single, and the girl or boy of your dreams can only go on a date with you on the day when you would normally rest, your act of faith may be to take a rain check. Whatever it takes, weekly practice of Sabbath should be a priority.

During this day of rest, we need to do our best to avoid normal work-week activities that contribute to our restlessness. This could mean turning off the computer or cell phone. This may result in no email, Facebook, Twitter, or

BuzzFeed for an entire day; I know you doubt me, but it really is possible. Once a week, we may have to avoid the office, set an "away" message for email, and not check voicemails. The laundry, the dishes, the garage, the bathroom (including the toilet used by four little boys), and the trash may have to wait for a day. Term papers may need to be written ahead of time, or be taken care of afterwards; the same goes for studying for an exam or for midterms. Balance the bank account or checkbook another day. Washing the car can wait.

While we are at it, allow me a moment to point out that I said "may" or "perhaps" a lot. The reason is that our goal is not to create a checklist. Again, we're naturally self-righteous, so checklists created to make sure we will rest can easily lead to restlessness. No, the list is there simply to help provoke the brainstorming process, so that we can better understand how to rest from what is normally considered work in our lives. Each person knows their routines and their rhythms and should act with them in mind. Each person also knows where the sacrifices will require faith. [Here's a hint: identify a non-essential thing or activity that you can't seem to live without, and then see what happens in your heart when you merely *consider* giving it up for a day. If you just died inside, you might want to think about letting it fall under Sabbath rest.]

Do you see how much faith something like this takes? We are used to operating at full capacity throughout the week, and we are terrified of what might happen if we abandoned all or part of that unsustainable pattern. What will that person think of me if I tell them "no"? How will I get a good grade if I give up one day a week in my studies? How will I have enough money to pay bills if I turn down that shift? What if I miss out on that business deal by not replying immediately? Will he or she ever agree to go out with me again if I tell them no, especially for such a "strange" reason?

Practicing Sabbath requires truckloads of faith. But, the nice thing to remember is that the object (i.e. Person) of that faith is perfectly capable of taking care of each and every one of our needs. Practicing Sabbath is refreshing for our souls. When we choose to take a break once a week, we trust that all of these needs have already been met through Christ, whether we see it yet or not. The work has already been completed by Him, whether actually or effectively (by way of promise). Weekly Sabbath is a tangible reminder of that truth. Therefore, you and I are choosing to pause and rest and trust Him.

When we physically stop our works, we are more readily able to remember the lessons of the Gospel. We are quicker to recall that God has already worked fully and completely on our behalf, that He has done what we were not sufficient to do in-and-of ourselves. We are choosing to remember the ancient truth, "Since he did not spare even his own Son, but gave him up for us all, won't he also give us everything else?" (Rom 8:32, NLT). The practice of Sabbath helps us to do that.

I believe that the actual day on which we choose to do this is up to the individual or family. We are *not* free to be led by our selfish preferences or by convenience alone but, instead, are free to choose a day that works best for our resting in Jesus. The chosen day is far less important than our conscious decision to be intentional and act in faith. As such, just pick a day and prepare to stop your labors. Some are convinced that it needs to happen on a Sunday, what is traditionally known in the Church as "the Lord's day." Others view it as needing to happen on some portion of Saturday, which is the traditional Jewish Sabbath. Others take this day in the middle of the week, or whenever they can simply make it happen in their busy work schedules. Some are able to practice on the same day every week, while others have to shift it to a different day every week. Some may have to start with only part of a day, while they work out on-the-fly how to eventually make it happen for a full day.

I believe the Bible provides us with a lot of flexibility in this. Consider another of the Apostle Paul's letters:

> *So don't let anyone condemn you for what you eat or drink, or for not celebrating certain holy days or new moon ceremonies or Sabbaths. For these rules are only shadows of the reality yet to come. And Christ himself is that reality.* (Col 2:16-17, NLT)

Shadows are not the thing themselves. The most important thing isn't the shadow, but the thing itself. The practice of Sabbath is a shadow that points to a present and future reality with Jesus. Don't worship the Sabbath; worship Jesus. And be committed to trusting God's comprehensive provision by faith:

> *One person esteems one day as better than another, while another esteems all days alike. Each one should be fully convinced in his own mind. The one who observes the day, observes it in honor of the Lord. The one who eats, eats in honor of the Lord, since he gives thanks to God, while the one who abstains, abstains in honor of the Lord and gives thanks to God.* (Rom 14:5-6, ESV)

Whatever you choose, do so in faith. Otherwise, the whole point is missed.

On Seasonal Sabbath

A seasonal Sabbath involves anything past one week:

monthly, quarterly, annually, and so on. I have heard of some who plan on a long weekend once a month or quarter, in order to take a prayer retreat or simply to refresh as a family. This can also include a professional Sabbatical once every five to ten years. Similarly, this can include planning retreats or actual vacations. There's a lot of flexibility here as well.

While there is certainly some importance to the activities that you permit or forgo during this time, there is a greater importance on the state of your heart—its motivations and its source of rest. Why are you choosing to rest? What are you resting from? Why are you able to rest, even in the face of responsibilities, deadlines, etc.? How is this rest reminding me of God's provision in the Gospel? How is rest reminding me of God's care over every area of my life? These (and more) are questions that need to be asked.

Regarding a professional Sabbatical, we are talking about a significant length of time (e.g. weeks or months) to take a rest from your work. Accordingly, there needs to be much care, prayer, agreement, and planning on how best to prepare for and enter into a season like this. It should not be done lightly. For those who have actually taken a Sabbatical, however, most will tell you that it was well worth the trouble of planning it out. I have come across some accounts indicating that it was timely and even life-saving for their personal, family, marriage, professional, and/or ministry health. There are already many books and resources out there to help plan a wisely timed, effective, and restorative Sabbatical, so I will leave it to them to do so.

An Example of Practicing Weekly Sabbath

Concepts are great but, if you're anything like me, you

may have a hard time envisioning what this could look like for you personally. Therefore, I will utilize this final section to do what someone once did for me. I am grateful to God for the ministry of Kyle and Christine Hoover, for Kyle at one point took a lengthy amount of time to share with me how they have tried to practice resting as a family one day a week. The timing of his advice could not have been better, too, as I was reeling at the time in my role as first-time student pastor. All told, the principles, ideas, and creativity helped lay the groundwork for what we do today. We adapted what they shared with us, and I fully anticipate and welcome readers to do the same as I share our family's (current) Sabbath routines.

Our day of practicing Sabbath tends to be on the same day every week, depending on the season that we are in—we have previously utilized Monday, Friday, Saturday, and Sunday. Even in saying this, there have also been times where we've had to shift it one week because there was something that we simply needed to make room for. It happens.

Apart from one year, a year that was therefore tougher than it needed to be, our family has sought to practice Sabbath once a week ever since 2006. All these years, we have seen God faithfully love, care for, and provide for our family through the exercise of practicing Sabbath. This includes seasons of salary and of hourly pay; before kids and in the midst of parenthood; while working in the for-profit and in the non-profit sectors; in years of abundance and of living paycheck-to-paycheck; while serving in a direct ministry roles as well as in supporting roles; in times when we ate surf 'n' turf and when we weren't sure how we were going to make rent. So, I'm here to tell you it can be done.

Our Sabbath day typically begins with a breakfast of

some kind, maybe with some light Bible reading (individually or as a family). Afterwards, I will take the kids out for about three to four hours for what we affectionately call "daddy-kiddo time." This is my opportunity to engage in some focused and extended quality time with my children. We have enjoyed all kinds of things together: getting donuts or pancakes; going swimming; playing at a park; visiting a local zoo or aquarium; hiking; taking a ferry ride; and so on.

Because we are out and about, this also means that my lovely wife, Julie, gets to enjoy that time alone with the Lord. She has spent this time in all kinds of ways—Bible reading and meditation; journaling; prayer; getting out and taking a walk; knitting or crocheting while listening to sermon podcasts; and even taking a long nap. All of these things point her to being refreshed and at rest in Jesus and His Gospel.

Afterwards, Julie and the kids have lunch together, while I sometimes take a quick power-nap of about half an hour. I then head out for what is regularly my favorite time of the week. For about two to four hours, I will sit at a coffee shop and enjoy some Bible reading, journaling, prayer, confession of sin, and other spiritual disciplines. On occasion, I will listen to worship songs in other languages, as this can help me emotionally connect to God's missionary "heart." I almost always have a Christian or missionary biography with me during this time; these have been a source of great personal encouragement and refreshment. I have even used this time to write down some poetry or song lyrics that reflect my personal experience with the Lord. Meanwhile, Julie and the kids are typically enjoying some quality time at the house—playing, drawing, quiet time, etc.

After I finish my "coffee with Jesus," I will typically

pick up pizza, and our family will enjoy a movie night or, less frequently, a board-game night. After playing with the kids a bit more—at this point in the evening, it is usually wrestling, hide-and-seek, or random silly song creation time—and after putting them to bed, Julie and I get some alone time.

We often begin that time by talking and praying together, usually for about an hour. If family (i.e. free child-care) is around, we will sometimes do this during a walk. Afterwards, we may play a board game, watch a TV show or movie, read a book, or just head to bed early. This has been our pattern for several years, and it has regularly refreshed us and pointed us to being at-rest in the completed works of Christ. With four kids and bills to pay, there is always something we could be doing. But, instead, we choose to rest from those things and trust that God will provide for any and all needs, because He has already provided for our greatest need in the Gospel.

Naturally, this time will look different for everyone. A person's stage of life will affect how the day is spent. A person's occupation will likewise have bearing on this. For example, professions in the healthcare industry, the public or government sector, or the military may have to get creative. We should not forget those who are in prison (Heb 13:3), regardless of the reason they are there, but especially if they are part of the persecuted church. I will not pretend to know what practicing Sabbath looks like for them, but I am biblically convinced that God's rest is avail-able and that He is fully able to lead such ones in how to practice it in their highly unique situation. For everyone, another important consideration is one's physical, spiritual, and emotional needs. Remember that people are refreshed in different ways. Some will want to spend time out in nature, while others prefer to be surrounded by concrete.

And that's okay. All of this and more should be considered when intentionally planning to practice Sabbath.

While I highly recommend that some of that time be spent with the Bible and in prayer—after all, how can we be at rest in God's promises if we don't even know what they are?—I will not go so far as to say how much time. Each needs to find a refreshing rhythm that is also motivated by faith and truth.

Whatever you do, make sure that your ambition is rest in Jesus and in His Gospel. The goal is to walk away from the week's practice of Sabbath having truly met with the Lord. We can easily deceive ourselves, which is why being intentional with the time is so important. Engage in things that will help you to remember that God's work on your behalf is complete. Try to avoid things that will likely distract you from this type of meditation or provoke a restless spirit in your heart. What are some intentional ways that you can connect with God? What will truly refresh you? How is God leading you to rest in Him?

I hope this exploration of rest, of the Sabbath and the Gospel, has been a transforming experience for you, as it has been for me. I hope this has not come across as a pretentious attempt at superiority or of knowledge, because that would break my heart. Instead, I desire that you have beheld Christ and His Gospel through the lens of the Sabbath (and vice versa), and that you have found them altogether more beautiful and satisfying than you could ever have imagined. In short, I hope and pray that you have found the rest that you have long been looking for, the rest that you were made for.

I truly believe that God intended for the Sabbath and the Gospel to go together. In the Gospel, God has promised to give us rest from our works through the completed work of Christ. And, in the Sabbath, God has reminded us to pause and reflect both on our great need for this Gospel as well as on His faithful provision of it. Indeed, it is through Jesus that we find all of our needs met, including our need for rest itself (Mt 11:28-30).

One of my favorite quotes on the topic of rest comes

from St. Augustine, a man who had to learn and apply these truths long ago just as we have to today. In many ways, it summarizes all that has been written here, but only needs a sentence or two to do so. In pondering Christ, this early church father once said: "You move us to delight in praising You; for You have made us for Yourself, and our hearts are restless until they find their rest in You."[1]

May God's grace lead us more and more to discover what it means to truly find our rest in Him. Amen.

ACKNOWLEDGMENTS

While this work is dedicated to God, I also have much gratitude to Him for the many that were a part of this journey with me. First, to my beloved bride and best friend, Julie, this book would not have been possible without your faithful and patient love, support, and encouragement. To my children: Benjamin, Jonathan (R.I.P.), Abigail, Lillian, and Tobias—may you forever find rest in the love and completed works of Jesus Christ.

I am indebted to my parents, Bryan and Margaret Ferguson, whom God chose to raise me. They have loved me well throughout my life, into adulthood and into my own fatherhood. Even if they had not—though they certainly did!—they are deserving of honor simply because they are my parents. I am grateful to God, my heavenly Father, for teaching me this lesson in 2007 when He enabled me to see and to repent of the grave and long-standing sin of dishonoring my parents. I also want to give due honor to my parents-in-law, Bill and Denice Fisher, who similarly loved their daughter well. These two brave souls not only let a homely and bearded 23-year old with a camo-painted truck marry their daughter, they also welcomed me into their family as a son.

I also want to sincerely thank those who read, gave feedback on, and provided some editing for early drafts of this book: Julie Ferguson, Margaret Ferguson, Denice Fisher, Ron Pracht, Andrew Thomasson, Margaret Fitzgerald, Greg Pickering, Mark Straznicky, and Marcia Rebrovich. This book certainly would not have been completed, nor would it have been readable, without your sacrificial service in the Lord towards me.

More broadly, to the many who have invested in my life and in my walking with Jesus over the years, some "planting" and others "watering" all while God was "causing the growth" (1 Cor 3:6), may you be encouraged that your labors were and are never in vain (1 Cor 15:58). If God can save and transform this great sinner into the image of His Son, then there is always hope for others of those in whom you are investing.

Lastly, to the pastors, missionaries, ministry leaders, deacons, and other servants of the Gospel around the world who have or will somehow come across this book, I sincerely thank you for serving the Lord and for carrying such a special burden—"[going] out for the sake of the Name" (3 Jn 1:7-8). Regardless of whether or not we have met, or ever will meet in this life, I especially thought of you when writing this book. I considered the remote possibility that perhaps a small handful of you might be encouraged by it; and this possibility, coupled with the general desire to be found faithful myself, helped push me forward with the many stages of this process. By the grace of God, I humbly remind and exhort you to let your works be done in faith, as joyfully as possible, and always out of a heart of rest in the finished work of our Lord Jesus.

BIBLIOGRAPHY

Arthur, Andrew. "Week 1: Acts 1:1-2:47." *Movement: An 8-Week Communal Study of the Book of Acts*. Seattle: The Hallows Church, 2011.

Augustine of Hippo and Schaff, Philip, ed. *The Confessions and Letters of St. Augustin with a Sketch of His Life and Work*. Vol. 1. A Select Library of the Nicene and Post-Nicene Fathers of the Christian Church, First Series. Buffalo: Christian Literature Company, 1886.

Baab, Lynne M. *Sabbath Keeping: Finding Freedom in the Rhythms of Rest*. Downers Gove: InterVarsity Press, 2005.

Biblical Financial Study: Small Group Student Manual. Knoxville: Crown Financial Ministries, 2006.

Brooks, James A. *Mark*. Vol. 23. The New American Commentary. Nashville: Broadman & Holman Publishers, 1991.

Cash, Johnny. "No Earthly Good," from *The Rambler*. New York City: Columbia Records, 1977.

Cole, R. Alan. *Mark: An Introduction and Commentary*. Vol. 2. Tyndale New Testament Commentaries. Downers Grove, IL: InterVarsity Press, 1989.

"Deforestation Facts, Information, and Effects." *National Geographic*. Accessed: October 6, 2017. <http://www.nationalgeographic.com/environment/global-warming/deforestation/>

Edwards, Jonathan. "To Deborah Hatheway" in *Letters and Personal Writings*, ed. George S. Claghorn, vol. 16 of *The Works of Jonathan Edwards*. New Haven: Yale University Press, 1998. 92-93.

Elliot, Elisabeth. *These Strange Ashes*. Ann Arbor: Servant Publications, 1998.

Fritz, Mike. "Take a 360 degree stroll through a 'Trash Mountain.'" *PBS Network*. May 9, 2017. <http://www.pbs.org/newshour/updates/take-360-degree-stroll-trash-mountain/>

Gaffigan, Jim. *Dad Is Fat*. New York: Three Rivers Press, 2013.

Garrels, Josh and Epipheo Studios. "Words Remain - Epipheo Remix." *YouTube*, uploaded by Josh Garrels, 17 Jan 2017, <https://www.youtube.com/watch?v=WQgl12_btSQ>.

Gomez, Alan. "Here are all the victims of the Las Vegas shooting." *USA Today*. Oct 6, 2017. <https://www.usatoday.com/story/news/nation/2017/10/06/here-all-victims-las-vegas-shooting/733236001/>

Greear, J. D. *Gospel: Recovering the Power that Made Christianity Revolutionary*. Nashville: B&H Publishing Group, 2011.

Keller, Timothy. *Center Church: Doing Balanced, Gospel-Centered Ministry in Your City*. Grand Rapids: Zondervan, 2012.

Keller, Timothy. *The Prodigal God: Recovering the Heart of the Christian Faith*. New York: Penguin Books, 2008.

Keller, Timothy, and Kathy Keller. *The Meaning of*

Marriage: Facing the Complexities of Commitment with the Wisdom of God. New York: Dutton, 2011.

Loconte, Joseph. *A Hobbit, a Wardrobe, and a Great War: How J. R. R. Tolkien and C. S. Lewis Rediscovered Faith, Friendship, and Heroism in the Cataclysm of 1914–1918*. Nashville: Nelson Books. 2015.

Lewis, C.S. (Clive Staples). *The Great Divorce*. New York: HaperCollins Publishers, 2001.

Lewis, C. S. (Clive Staples). *The Magician's Nephew*. New York: Harper Trophy, 2000.

Lloyd-Jones, Sally. *The Jesus Storybook Bible: Every Story Whispers His Name*. Grand Rapids: Zonderkidz, 2007.

Luther, Martin. *The Bondage of the Will*. Translation by Henry Cole, 1823. CCEL: Christian Classics Ethereal Library. <http://www.ccel.org/ccel/luther/bondage.ix.xvii.html>

Marsden, George M. *Jonathan Edwards: A Life*. New Haven: Yale University Press, 2003.

Mathews, K. A. "Genesis 1-11:26". Vol. 1A, *The New American Commentary*. Nashville: Broadman & Holman Publishers, 1996.

McMillan, John Mark. "Death in His Grave," from *The Medicine*. Colorado Springs: Integrity Media, 2010.

Nee, Watchman. *Sit, Walk, Stand*. Carol Stream: Tyndale House Publishers, Inc, 1977.

New American Standard Bible: 1995 Update. LaHabra: The Lockman Foundation, 1995.

Pierre-Louis, Kendra. "Guess how many giant patches of garbage there are in the ocean now?" *Popular Science*. July 21, 2017. <https://www.popsci.com/south-pacific-garbage-patch>

Piper, John. *Let the Nations Be Glad!: The Supremacy of God in Missions, 3rd ed*. Grand Rapids: Baker Academic, 2010.

Rice, Chris. "Welcome to Our World," from *Deep Enough to Dream*. Nashville: Rocketown Records, 1997.

Sidder, Aaron. "Remember the Ozone Hole? Now There's Proof It's Healing." *National Geographic*. June 30, 2016. <http://news.nationalgeographic.com/2016/06/antarctic-ozone-hole-healing-fingerprints/>

Stott, J. R. W. *The Cross of Christ: 20th Anniversary Edition*. Downers Grove: InterVarsity Press, 2006.

Strong, James. *A Concise Dictionary of the Words in the Greek Testament and The Hebrew Bible*. Bellingham, WA: Logos Bible Software, 2009.

Swanson, James. *Dictionary of Biblical Languages with Semantic Domains: Hebrew (Old Testament)*. Oak Harbor: Logos Research Systems, Inc., 1997.

The Holy Bible: English Standard Version. Wheaton, IL: Crossway Bibles, 2016.

The Holy Bible: Holman Christian Standard Version. Nashville: Holman Bible Publishers, 2009.

The Joshua Project. 2018. <http://joshuaproject.net>

The Silence of the Lambs. Directed by Jonathan Demme. Los Angeles: Orion Pictures Corporation, 1991.

Tolkien, J.R.R. *The Fellowship of the Ring: Being the First Part of The Lord of the Rings*. New York: Houghton Mifflin Company, 1994.

Tozer, A.W. "On the Hammer, File, and Furnace," *The Root of the Righteous*. Pompton Plains: Christian Publications, 1986.

Tyndale House Publishers. *Holy Bible: New Living Translation*. Carol Stream, IL: Tyndale House Publishers, 2013.

United States Census Bureau. "U.S. and World Population Clock." *Census.gov*. October 31, 2017. <https://www.census.gov/popclock/>

Wait Until Dark. Directed by Terence Young. Burbank: Warner Home Video, 1967.

Wilson, Durenda. *The Unhurried Homeschooler: A Simple, Mercifully Short Book on Homeschooling*. CreateSpace Independent Publishing Platform. 2016.

Zumwalt, John Willis. *Passion for the Heart of God*. Choctaw: HGM Publishing, 2000.

NOTES

Prologue

1. Only God could orchestrate such a beautiful internal harmony! Again, the Bible does this beyond-magnificently with many themes. But, seeing as this is a book about rest, we will stick primarily with that one.

2. I used quotation marks here in an attempt to preserve the purest meaning of the term, used by missiologists, church leaders, and Christians to classify *truly* unreached people groups, most of whom are within what is known as the "10/40 Window." For this definition, please see *The Joshua Project* at joshuaproject.net. Nevertheless, I have chosen to utilize this term to add forcefulness to the unique —and, in my opinion, historically *pre*-Christian—state of spirituality in the Pacific Northwest.

3. Those who have lived in Seattle just chuckled because I have just described Seattle's weather for roughly seven to eight months out of the year. And when I say "chuckled," of course, I mean "laughed nervously and quasi-despairingly" with a cup of coffee in-hand.

4. Tozer, A.W. "On the Hammer, File, and Furnace," *The Root of the Righteous*. Pompton Plains: Christian Publications, 1986. 137.

5. So says the guy writing the book. Ha!

6. For some reason, that paragraph made me think of Bilbo Baggins: "I don't know half of you half as well as I should like; and I like less than half of you half as well as you deserve." Tolkien, J.R.R. *The Fellowship of the Ring: Being the First Part of The Lord of the Rings*. New York: Houghton Mifflin Company, 1994. 29.

7. Greear, J. D. *Gospel: Recovering the Power that Made Christianity Revolutionary*. Nashville: B&H Publishing Group, 2011. 21.

8. Inspiring, isn't it? That's probably another reason why I didn't make it very far at first.

9. I got this genius phrasing from the book, *The Unhurried Homeschooler: A Simple, Mercifully Short Book on Homeschooling*, by Durenda Wilson. CreateSpace Independent Publishing Platform. 2016.

10. Thank you, Troy and Beth Hamilton. As I've told to you often, your words stay with us.

1. The Sabbath and the Gospel, Part 1

1. We will get to why that matters in more detail in chapter three (and following) of this book.
2. Strong, James. "שַׁבָּת". *A Concise Dictionary of the Words in the Greek Testament and The Hebrew Bible*. Bellingham, WA: Logos Bible Software, 2009. 112.
3. Swanson, James. "שָׁבַת" *Dictionary of Biblical Languages with Semantic Domains: Hebrew (Old Testament)*. Oak Harbor: Logos Research Systems, Inc., 1997.
4. Though, the heft of this particular command is likely much more relatable for those in Eastern cultures than for those of us in Western ones. I have learned much from those cultures whose communal identities naturally leads to greater honor of father and mother (and elders). Those of us in the West have much to learn from those in the East in this regard, most especially those who are in Christ.
5. Strong, James. "εὐαγγέλιον" *A Concise Dictionary of the Words in the Greek Testament and The Hebrew Bible*. Bellingham, WA: Logos Bible Software, 2009.
6. Lloyd-Jones, Sally. *The Jesus Storybook Bible: Every Story Whispers His Name*. Grand Rapids: Zonderkidz, 2007. 14.

2. The Death Penalty and the Sabbath

1. More precisely, in Exodus 16:23-30, which will be studied later on in chapter seven.
2. I chose these two books because of context. By this, I mean their literary "proximity" to the Ten Commandments, where the Sabbath was handed down among the Law. These books are where one might find many of these penalties described.
3. This is an example of where the reader needs to remember the scope and limitations of this work. There was a lot to that sentence, and I'm sure there are entire books out there dedicated to either proving or disproving the statement. But, again, that is not what we are after here. So, please stay the course.
4. Yes, this still happens in some places.
5. Regarding the matter of valuation between a person and an animal, God certainly values the animals He created; but it is consistently clear throughout the Bible that He values the life of people far more than that of animals. This isn't wrong of God to do so, and we have the same type of practice. Stealing someone's pet dog is not punished the same way as stealing a car or, God forbid, stealing another human being. Though, there are a number

of indications in Western culture that we value pets more than other people. Shame on us.

6. Please, please, please do not interpret this as, "We should lay down the death penalty today for violating Sabbath practice." That is not what I am saying, so please do not go there. I am merely trying to help us understand the biblical importance of Sabbath.

3. The Creation and the Sabbath

1. For those with children, you especially know the pain of this dilemma!

2. This book assumes Adam and Eve to be real, literal people, from which every person on earth receives their lineage.

3. For a very fictional, yet still very beautiful, illustration of this creative scene, I recommend the chapter entitled "The Founding of Narnia," out of a children's book by C.S. Lewis, *The Magician's Nephew*. Lewis, C. S. (Clive Staples). *The Magician's Nephew*. New York: Harper Trophy, 2000. 112-123.

4. Adam and Eve and the Sabbath

1. For an exploration of the Gospel as a type of "homecoming" that humanity longs for—we are alienated from our true home (i.e. Eden), but are given the opportunity to return through the blood of Jesus Christ—I eagerly recommend select portions of two Tim Keller works. The first is *The Prodigal God* (90-102), New York: Penguin Books, 2008. The second is *Center Church* (41-42), Grand Rapids: Zondervan, 2012.

2. This can tell us much about the inherently-positive (and not sinful) nature of work, but that is not quite the focus. I was initially introduced to this amazing truth by the work of Crown Financial Ministries. *Biblical Financial Study: Small Group Student Manual*. Knoxville: Crown Financial Ministries, 2006.

3. Strong, James. "שׁוֹם". *A Concise Dictionary of the Words in the Greek Testament and The Hebrew Bible*. Bellingham, WA: Logos Bible Software, 2009. 113.

4. Mathews, K. A. "2:15," from "Genesis 1-11:26". Vol. 1A, *The New American Commentary*. Nashville: Broadman & Holman Publishers, 1996.

5. Nee, Watchman. *Sit, Walk, Stand*. Carol Stream: Tyndale House Publishers, Inc, 1977. 4.

5. The Fall and the Sabbath

1. Keller, Timothy, and Kathy Keller. *The Meaning of Marriage: Facing the Complexities of Commitment with the Wisdom of God*. New York: Dutton, 2011. 101.

6. The Exodus and the Sabbath

1. So much awesomeness from the Lord God in the exodus events! And, this is to say nothing of the Passover, which is an equally important matter in the narrative. Alas, that subject falls outside this book's purpose of examining the exodus event. Therefore, we leave it to other books and teachers to instruct us.
2. E.g. Hapi, Isis, Ra, etc. And don't forget that the Pharaohs were also worshiped as gods in ancient Egypt.

7. The Manna and the Sabbath

1. If you're looking for a laugh and a mere glimpse into how volatile the wilderness wandering experience could have been at times, visit YouTube for the various SNICKERS® commercials with the tagline, "You're not you when you're hungry." My bizarre sense of humor imagines the sum total of roughly one million Joe Pescis, Danny Trejos, Betty Whites, Bobcat Goldthwaits, Aretha Franklins, Willem Dafoes, and Mr. Beans all interacting in the desert.

8. Mt. Sinai and the Sabbath

1. As a brief aside, this line of thinking should terrify us Westerners into repentance as we consider the similarly-weighty command to "Honor your father and mother," a violation of which also resulted in death.
2. Along these lines, I cannot be eager enough to recommend two books that were, for me, literally life-changing: *Passion for the Heart of God*, by John Willis Zumwalt (Choctaw: HGM Publishing, 2000) and *Let the Nations Be Glad!: The Supremacy of God in Missions*, by John Piper (3rd ed., Grand Rapids: Baker Academic, 2010).
3. Keller, Timothy. *The Prodigal God: Recovering the Heart of the Christian Faith*. New York: Penguin Books, 2008. 44-45.

9. The Sign and Covenant of the Sabbath

1. United States Census Bureau. "U.S. and World Population Clock." *Census.gov.* October 31, 2017. <https://www.census.gov/popclock/>
2. This back-and-forth reminds me of a powerful image developed by way of allegory in the C.S. Lewis book, *The Great Divorce* (106-115), New York: HaperCollins Publishers, 2001. One story portrays a character's battle with sin and lust, personified as a red lizard, and his uncertainty in whether or not he truly wants to let it go.
3. Swanson, James. "קָדַשׁ" *Dictionary of Biblical Languages with Semantic Domains: Hebrew (Old Testament).* Oak Harbor: Logos Research Systems, Inc., 1997.
4. Swanson, James. "בְּרִית" *Dictionary of Biblical Languages with Semantic Domains : Hebrew (Old Testament).* Oak Harbor: Logos Research Systems, Inc., 1997.
5. Arthur, Andrew. "Week 1: Acts 1:1-2:47." *Movement: An 8-Week Communal Study of the Book of Acts.* Seattle: The Hallows Church, 2011. 5.
6. Or, as the Song of Solomon says it, "My lover is mine, and I am his" (2:16, NLT).
7. Baab, Lynne M. *Sabbath Keeping: Finding Freedom in the Rhythms of Rest.* Downers Gove: InterVarsity Press, 2005. 17-18.

10. The Promised Land and the Sabbath

1. Every book deserves multiple, and, in this particular case, *obscure*, pop-culture references. If you got this one, you inevitably must be a bit of a weirdo and music junkie like me.
2. Don't get too caught up on the phrase "inactivity of rest" just yet. It should make more sense the farther along you progress in the book, which even includes a practical exploration at the end.

11. The Prophets and the Sabbath

1. E.g. Isaiah 58:13-14; Jeremiah 17:19-27; Ezekiel 20:1-22; and Amos 8:1-14
2. Please pardon the inherent and unfortunate pun.
3. Fittingly, this very illustration will be explored more in the next chapter.

12. The Exile and the Sabbath

1. Remember Him, from the Garden of Eden?

13. Jesus and the Sabbath: God as Servant

1. This phrase comes from the Chris Rice song, "Welcome to Our World." The song itself, the lyrics, and the story behind them are quite beautiful. Rice, Chris. "Welcome to Our World," from *Deep Enough to Dream*. Nashville: Rocketown Records, 1997.
2. I must humbly confess that I have learned the hard way (on more than one occasion) that never do I feel farther from God than when I am thinking, believing, and living self-righteously like a Pharisee. And, unsurprisingly, these seasons have coincided with times where my faith has been most repugnant to others, both near and far, and to myself.
3. Cf. Ex 25:30; 35:13; 39:36; Lev 24:5-9
4. Brooks, James A. *Mark*. Vol. 23. The New American Commentary. Nashville: Broadman & Holman Publishers, 1991. 66.
5. Cole, R. Alan. *Mark: An Introduction and Commentary*. Vol. 2. Tyndale New Testament Commentaries. Downers Grove, IL: InterVarsity Press, 1989. 130.
6. As it pertains to Jesus and His kingdom, the phrase "Son of Man" is loaded with meaning (cf. Daniel 7:9-14).
7. This portion of Matthew is examined in the next chapter.

14. Jesus and the Sabbath: God as Healer

1. For further development of this idea, see the chapter, "Jesus and the Sabbath: God as King."
2. R.I.P. Stuart Orlando Scott, renowned American sports analyst during my youth.
3. Gaffigan, Jim. *Dad Is Fat*. New York: Three Rivers Press, 2013. 264
4. I am not ignorant of the fact that this still happens in certain parts of the world today. By God's grace, may He help His people to continue to "go" to the furthest reaches of the earth with the Gospel and with Gospel-fueled works of mercy and compassion and healing.
5. Perhaps it is better to humbly remember that we all act the same way sometimes, only with different things.
6. Creating a meaningful contemporary portrayal of this story has to be rather challenging but, in this author's opinion, credit to Epipheo Studios who, under the commission of the executive

producers at My Free Bible, succeeded in doing this with their remix and animation of Josh Garrels' song, "Words Remain," which on its own is also quite powerful. Garrels, Josh and Epipheo Studios. "Words Remain - Epipheo Remix." *YouTube*, uploaded by Josh Garrels, 17 Jan 2017, <https://www.youtube.com/watch?v=WQgl12_btSQ>.

15. Jesus and the Sabbath: God as Light

1. *The Silence of the Lambs.* Directed by Jonathan Demme. Los Angeles: Orion Pictures Corporation, 1991.
2. *Wait Until Dark.* Directed by Terence Young. Burbank: Warner Home Video, 1967.
3. Parents will definitely get this one. However, this LEGO® matter is probably the only exception on the list. No matter what you do, there will always be remnants of these foot-piercing weapons of mass destruction lurking in the shadows.

16. Jesus and the Sabbath: God as Savior

1. This is explored in greater detail in the chapter, "Jesus and the Sabbath: God as King."
2. Luther, Martin. *The Bondage of the Will.* Translation by Henry Cole, 1823. CCEL: Christian Classics Ethereal Library. <http://www.c-cel.org/ccel/luther/bondage.ix.xvii.html >

17. Jesus and the Sabbath: God as Sacrifice

1. One I highly recommend is *The Cross of Christ*, although I must also mention that I do not agree with some of the author's conclusions (later in life) regarding annihilationism. Stott, J. R. W. *The Cross of Christ: 20th Anniversary Edition.* Downers Grove: InterVarsity Press, 2006.

18. Jesus and the Sabbath: God as Life

1. McMillan, John Mark. "Death in His Grave," from *The Medicine.* Colorado Springs: Integrity Media, 2010.

19. Jesus and the Sabbath: God as King

1. I'm assuming it is a safe bet to say that, in every year of every generation, one could say this.

2. Gomez, Alan. "Here are all the victims of the Las Vegas shooting." *USA Today*. Oct 6, 2017. <https://www.usatoday.com/story/news/nation/2017/10/06/here-all-victims-las-vegas-shooting/733236001/>

3. This is addressed in greater detail in the next chapter, "The New Creation and The Sabbath."

4. To name only a very few, and thereby create a woefully abbreviated list, we are humanly indebted to the influence and work of people like: William Wilberforce and Frederick Douglas during the slave trade eras in Great Britain and America, respectively; Dr. Martin Luther King, Jr. and Dorothy Height during the American Civil Rights Era; Nelson Mandela during the era of apartheid in South Africa; Mother Theresa among the indescribably impoverished of India; and the ten Boom family and an unknown number of others who risked their lives giving refuge to the Jews during the Holocaust.

5. What an indictment against us! As image-bearers, we have the amazing capability to create from the resources of the world that God made. And, yet, we take these resources and make implements of death. For a very brief excursus on facets of this in the World War I era, I recommend the first chapter of Joseph Loconte's book, *A Hobbit, a Wardrobe, and a Great War: How J. R. R. Tolkien and C. S. Lewis Rediscovered Faith, Friendship, and Heroism in the Cataclysm of 1914–1918*, entitled "The Funeral of a Great Myth." It is sobering as it casts light on the tragic consequences of the overly-hopeful *zeitgeist* of "human progress," which is eventually considered an illusion by the author.

6. Cash, Johnny. "No Earthly Good," from *The Rambler*. New York City: Columbia Records, 1977. Regarding this (un-) popular sentiment, I think it is pretty obvious that the "Man in Black" was bringing a rightful charge against those whose so-called profession of faith in Christ was nothing but empty religion and platitudes. That is, they appeared to care about God and the things of God, but that was grievously betrayed by the observation that they cared nothing for their fellow humanity. For an explanation, consider James 2:12-26. Nevertheless, even if my interpretation of these lyrics were incorrect, and even if the same negative view were held by some, it would be misinformed when one such person considers Jesus Christ. There was not, and is not, nor will there ever be, one person in all of history more *heavenly minded* than Jesus. And, appropriately so, there was, is, and will be none

who ever did more *earthly good* than He did. He is the epitome of the direct correlation between heavenly-mindedness and doing earthly good.

20. The New Creation and the Sabbath

1. Though, it is worth noting that the matter of stewardship *does* involve how we care for one another. The relationship between the two—stewardship and how we treat one another—is evident. Therefore, God help us to remember this when thinking about caring for what He has entrusted to us.
2. Pierre-Louis, Kendra. "Guess how many giant patches of garbage there are in the ocean now?" *Popular Science*. July 21, 2017. <https://www.popsci.com/south-pacific-garbage-patch>
3. Fritz, Mike. "Take a 360 degree stroll through a 'Trash Mountain.'" *PBS Network*. May 9, 2017. <http://www.pbs.org/newshour/updates/take-360-degree-stroll-trash-mountain/>
4. Sidder, Aaron. "Remember the Ozone Hole? Now There's Proof It's Healing." *National Geographic*. June 30, 2016. <http://news.nationalgeographic.com/2016/06/antarctic-ozone-hole-healing-fingerprints/>
5. "Deforestation Facts, Information, and Effects." *National Geographic*. Accessed: October 6, 2017. <http://www.nationalgeographic.com/environment/global-warming/deforestation/>
6. That is, anyone whose "name was not found written in the book of life" (Rev 20:15). Only those made new by Jesus—"those whose names are written in the Lamb's book of life" (21:27)—are allowed into this new world and into God's presence. The rest are cast into a terrible "lake of fire" (20:15) called Hell.

21. The Sabbath and the Gospel, Part 2

1. In fact, the ancient letter to the Hebrews as a whole has profound things to say about the heart and practice of Sabbath.

22. Practicing Sabbath: A Matter of Faith

1. Edwards, Jonathan. "To Deborah Hatheway" in *Letters and Personal Writings*, ed. George S. Claghorn, vol. 16 of *The Works of Jonathan Edwards*. New Haven: Yale University Press, 1998. 92-93.
2. Marsden, George M. *Jonathan Edwards: A Life*. New Haven: Yale University Press, 2003. 248-249.

3. Elliot, Elisabeth. *These Strange Ashes*. Ann Arbor: Servant Publications, 1998. 125-126.
4. A modern example of this is the "health-and-wealth gospel," which runs serious risk of this type of commoditizing and subsequent injury. Any gospel that does not call people to life in the grace of Christ is no gospel at all and comes with the severest of warnings (Gal 1:6-8).

23. Practicing Sabbath: Taking Action

1. For those who get the joke, you're welcome. . .
2. As a brief example, I believe that God is pleased when I treat my wife lovingly (1 Pet 3:7).

Epilogue

1. Augustine of Hippo and Schaff, Philip, ed. *The Confessions and Letters of St. Augustin with a Sketch of His Life and Work*. Vol. 1. A Select Library of the Nicene and Post-Nicene Fathers of the Christian Church, First Series. Buffalo, NY: Christian Literature Company, 1886. 45.

Printed in Great Britain
by Amazon

22584011R00109